Unity in Mission
A Bond of Peace for the Sake of Love

C. Andrew Doyle

I ask not only on behalf of these, but also on behalf of those who will believe in me through their word, that they may all be one. As you, Father, are in me and I am in you, may they also be in us, so that the world may believe that you have sent me. The glory that you have given me I have given them, so that they may be one, as we are one, I in them and you in me, that they may be completely one, so that the world may know that you have sent me and have loved them even has you have loved me.
John 17:20-23

Blessed are the peacemakers, for they will be called children of God.

Matthew 5:9

CONTENTS

Acknowledgments   i

1   Remarks by Secretary James A. Baker III   1

2   Choosing Unity   Pg 5

3   The Future We Create   Pg 10

4   The Responsibility of Bishops as Leader   Pg 18

5   Unity as an Instrument of Communion   Pg 25

6   Essential Foundations of Marriage   Pg 46

7   We Are Not of One Mind   Pg 67

8   A Communal Process   Pg 89

9   A Strategy for Unity in Mission   Pg 94

10   On Pilgrimage Together   Pg 99

11   Forward Into Mission   Pg162

ACKNOWLEDGMENTS

I am grateful for the many people who have spent time with me over these past seven years and shared their hopes and desires as well as their concerns and prayers. A number of these have been bishops who have shared in their thoughts and have supported me in discerning my leadership on this issue. I give thanks for the direction and clarity with which the following have offered guidance: the Most Rev. Justin Welby, the Most Rev. Rowan Williams, the Most Rev. Katharine Jefferts Schori, the Most Rev. George Carey, the Rt. Rev. James Tengatenga, the Rt. Rev. Philip Poole, the Rt. Rev. Ed Little, the Rt. Rev. Neil Alexander, and the Rt. Rev. Duncan Gray, III. I give thanks also for the Rt. Rev. Canon Kenneth Kearon (former Secretary General of the Anglican Communion) and the Rev. John Peterson (former Secretary General of the Anglican Communion). I give thanks for the Very Rev. Joe D. Reynolds (former dean of Christ Church Cathedral, Houston), the Rev. Dr. Russell Levenson (rector of St. Martin's, Houston), the Rev. Dr. Ian Markham (Dean of Virginia Theological Seminary), the Rev. Dr. Bill Stafford (former Dean of the Sewanee School of Theology), and the Rev. Dr. Paul Zahl (former Dean of Trinity School for Ministry, Ambridge) and the Rev. Larry Hall (former rector of St. John's the Divine, Houston).

I am thankful for the challenge and support that I have also received from Ms. Laurie Eiserloh (parishioner at St. David's, Austin). In no way do I mean to imply their endorsement of this paper, but I appreciate the time and conversations they have had with me over the last several years and their encouragement in seeking a way for the Diocese of Texas, and for the wider church, to seek unity globally.

In addition, these faithful bishops—the Rt. Rev. Claude E. Payne (seventh Bishop of Texas), the Rt. Rev. Don Wimberly (eighth Bishop of Texas), the Rt. Rev. Dena A. Harrison (bishop suffragan in the Diocese of Texas), the Rt. Rev. Jeff Fisher (bishop suffragan in the Diocese of Texas), and the Rt. Rev. Rayford B. High (bishop suffragan in the Diocese of Texas, retired)—all have been a part of this conversation and have offered nothing but their support of me for the sake of unity and the health of mission for the Diocese of Texas.

Most especially, I am thankful to the Rev. David Puckett and the Rev. Chris Bowhay, who agreed to help with editing the text, and Dr. Scott Bader-Saye, who agreed to serve on the Task Force for Unity and also agreed to be a reader for this paper. His thoughts have been most helpful in insuring a solid theological footing. Together they were my first readers.

I am also grateful for the Diocese of Texas staff who has helped me to make time devoted to this project. I am especially indebted to the Rev. Canons John Logan and John Newton, and Carol E. Barnwell, each of whom has helped with my thinking and my writing.

Let me now thank JoAnne, my wife. She is my partner in the adventure that is bishop. She has read more than a few pieces of my work, and in all she has given me her support despite the numbers of comma and semicolon corrections. I love her and am blessed to have her in my life.

Lastly, I am grateful to God and the people of the Diocese of Texas who have inspired my ministry and have invited me, as the ninth bishop diocesan, to share their lives. Their courage, their fierce tenacity for mission, and their belief in the kingdom of God—all of this makes me want to be a better bishop. Moreover, their audacity for the Gospel of Jesus Christ urges me to leadership on this issue.

1 REMARKS BY
SECRETARY JAMES A. BAKER III

At the inaugural meeting of our Episcopal Diocese of Texas Unity in Mission Task Force Meeting in 2011, Secretary Baker made the following remarks regarding sexuality issues facing the Church.

I became involved in this issue about three years ago, as we were witnessing the schism in The Episcopal Church over this issue play out in the form of one congregation after another leaving to go its own way. We were witnessing at that time as well—and before, frankly—the proliferation of lawsuits over church property that accompanied those departures. I personally grew quite concerned.

I really felt that we were desperately in need of a way to resolve our differences, rather than to allow those differences to continue to separate us. I tried to look at it from several different perspectives—first, as an Episcopalian, and one who dearly loves our Church, albeit one who really claims no expertise whatsoever in the polity of the Church. I will confess to you that I've learned a little about it, since I first became so concerned, but I really don't know a lot about the polity of the Church.

Secondly, I looked at it as someone who has had extensive experience in both national and international politics and negotiations. From both perspectives, it was clear to me that this issue is one that is so very divisive and with respect to which positions of both sides are so deeply held, that we're not going to resolve it, if we insist that we have to go one way or the other. That is, if we insist, that on this issue, there is going to be one winner and one loser. I must confess to you that I ran into a few of those types of issues during my time in public service that are so divisive that they're just not capable of being solved on a one-win, one-lose basis.

Instead I felt—and I still feel—very deeply that our goal ought to be to come up with a win-win solution, if we can, that gives those with views on either side of this issue, the opportunity still—notwithstanding their views—to dedicate their lives to Jesus Christ through The Episcopal Church. Now, saying that, I recognize and I appreciate that there will be some on the fringes of this issue that feel so committed and so dedicated that they will always look at this issue as an either-or matter. I just happen to think that continuing on that path is a recipe for disaster. My experience, frankly, told me that the best way to find that win-win solution would be to see if we couldn't create a system that allows both sides of the controversy to simply agree to disagree, and in so doing, to still maintain respect for one another in the process.

The more I thought about it, the more I felt that we should try to establish what might be called an all-are-welcome approach that allows our parishes to make important decisions on this issue. That seemed to me to be a fair and reasonable approach. It still seems to me to be a fair and reasonable approach. On this one issue, some will choose a more traditional stance, while others will choose to do blessings (and or marriages). Doing this—I think—allows the local parishes to make the critical decisions on the issues, and that is, after all—at least, in my view—consistent with the Church's long history of allowing for decision-making at the local levels.

As many—as all of you probably know—many of the same people who developed our country after the American Revolution—that is, Thomas Jefferson and George Washington and James Madison—were members of our Church after it separated from the The Church Of England. The system that those American Anglicans put into place was really not dissimilar to the democratic approach our founding fathers put into place. Yes—I guess—we'd have to acknowledge that the system has created some conflict, just as there are tensions in our country today between states' rights and federal rights, there is tension inside our Church between dioceses, The Episcopal Church, and the General Convention.

Overall, it is my view that the system has served our Church well for almost two and a half centuries, just as it has served our country well. Eventually, I discussed this idea with local and state and national Episcopal leaders. I was then asked to write an op-ed for the Virginia Theological Seminary that outlined my thinking, and I did that. For a variety of reasons, our Episcopal Church leaders said that they did not think this all-are-welcome or agree-to-disagree approach could be implemented at General Convention. I understand that, and, frankly, I agree with it, but I did get positive feedback from Episcopal leaders from several states, and particularly from Bishop Andy Doyle.

Now, Bishop Doyle has taken that article and thought prayerfully about it and refined it in many, many ways and made it much, much, much better. He will go through that in some detail shortly. I'm sure he has probably already discussed it with those of you who were there in Austin. First of all, what I want to say—and I'll say this in conclusion, if I might—is that I think we Episcopalians in Texas have an opportunity here to lead by example on this issue. That is, lead by example within The Episcopal Church in the United States. Frankly, if we were able to do that satisfactorily and effectively, it would be a lesson that, quite frankly, our national political leaders could learn a little bit from.

Hopefully, the approach that the Bishop is going to outline will serve as a textbook example that could demonstrate to dioceses elsewhere that, with mutual respect and understanding, we can adopt a process or a procedure or a policy, with respect to this very divisive issue, that will permit our Church to stay together during this understandably trying time. I happen to personally believe that our savior Jesus Christ would prefer us to come together with a solution to this issue that, irrespective of which side we may be on, will permit us to continue to be in communion with each other. Once again, let me simply say thanks to all of you for being willing to offer to try and find a way forward that can help our Church stay together and help it to concentrate on our common commitment to our Lord Jesus Christ and to the mission of his Church.

In the wake of the rulings by the Supreme Court June 26, 2015, Secretary Baker added the following remarks.

A lot has happened since I made those remarks in September 2011.

First, Bishop Doyle issued his inaugural *Unity in Mission* statement seven months later, giving guidance to Texas congregations wrestling with the difficult challenges related to sexual orientation. In the three years since then, eight of these congregations have decided to adopt more liberal approaches to this issue while five congregations have taken a more traditional approach. More importantly, no Texas church has broken away during that time, reversing what had been a divisive trend.

Individual churches in Texas have learned that the "agree-to-disagree" or "all-are-welcome" approach affords them a choice in this matter. Rather than get stuck in a winner-take-all argument that leads to more and more congregations pulling away from The Episcopal Church, church members have found ways to further their dialogue and find common ground. By having a mechanism to resolve differences on this issue, they also gained the opportunity to re-focus on the many matters that unite us rather than the one that divides us. In doing so, we may not have fully settled the church's position, but we have increased our understanding of one another, and that is a critical component of a united church.

Second, the U.S. Supreme Court recently ruled that gay marriage is legal nationwide. That, of course, is a seminal ruling in American history, one that very well may open the doors to further changes in our society.

And third, a week after the Supreme Court decision, the Episcopal General Convention approved rites for gay and lesbian couples. This new position inside the church has set the stage for revisions to the Book of Common Prayer to include new rites for marriage in the future

The debate will likely continue inside our church about which path clergy, congregations and church leaders should take in the future -- and that discourse may grow louder and even more heated among we Episcopalians, just as it has among Americans in the aftermath of the Supreme Court decision. We should hope that this does not become an either/or debate that serves to threaten the unity of our church by forcing us to have winners and losers. There should be room for all of us in God's church.

As we move forward, the time is ripe for Episcopalians to consider taking Bishop Doyle's updated *Unity in Mission* approach to the national and international level. Admittedly, not everyone has been pleased with that process. As in politics, hardliners on both sides have complained about this approach. But in Texas, it has served to help ameliorate our schism. The process Bishop Doyle has put in place allows Episcopalians in Texas to respectfully agree to disagree. For the long-term health of the Episcopal Church, I hope that other church leaders see the wisdom of spreading *Unity in Mission* to the entire church.

In the Epistle to the Ephesians, it is argued that the new church established after the crucifixion of Jesus Christ should maintain the unity which Jesus's death symbolized. As it is written in Ephesians 4:1-3, "As a prisoner for the Lord, then, I urge you to live a life worthy of the calling you have received. Be completely humble and gentle; be patient, bearing with one another in love. Make every effort to keep the unity of the Spirit through the bond of peace." That is the approach that our entire church should take as we continue to address the challenges that lie ahead of us. If we maintain a humble and gentle approach with one another, and if we remain patient during this important discussion, our church has a great opportunity to grow stronger as we all move forward together in the spirit of the Lord.

— James A. Baker, III, July 10, 2015

2 CHOOSING UNITY

The Church has always wrestled with difference in opinions, theology, and deeply held beliefs about creation, God, and the living out of our faith. For 40 years The Episcopal Church has wrestled with sexuality and sex regarding ordination, and with sexuality and how it relates to the sacrament of marriage. In fact, all of the major denominations—and even non-denominational churches— have been having the same discussion.

In the wake of Evangelicals coming out in favor of accepting gay, lesbian, and transgender individuals into the church, and into covenants of fidelity through marriage, the cultural acceptance is changing quickly. The Supreme Court ruling and the wider church acceptance of marriage presses on those with what is now a minority view. Moreover, more than 21 countries have legal marriage for same-sex couples. While huge numbers of Asian Christians share a more western acceptance of same-sex relationships, still huge numbers of African Christians do not. The global trajectory is clear, while the Church will continue to wrestle globally with this issue for the next two decades.

In traditional dioceses like Texas, anxiety rises once again, as we approach a time of when differences of opinion will become the headlines of newspapers. Our Episcopal Church's General Convention will have met and will once again have taken up the topic of how to be faithful in a culture where tradition limits our mission. Within the Church, reports and liturgies are being prepared, which will usher in a new age of sacramental understanding about sexuality and marriage for The Episcopal Church. Some people in The Episcopal Church will welcome these actions while others will not. The Episcopal Church is finding its way in the midst of a cultural sea change. As it attempts to be faithful to its mission, the liturgical and theological changes will challenge the wider church and much of the Anglican Communion, and it will challenge the people of the Diocese of

Texas on several fronts if not prayerfully weighed and a response made.

The United States as a vast community of diverse opinions is also divided on the issue of marriage. States have been legalizing marriage for all people while others have retaliated by passing laws that keep their state free from such changes. This summer the United States Supreme Court ruled in favor of same sex marriage. Many believe, as I do, that the legalization of same-sex marriage will create further confusion in our Episcopal communities. I believe it is just to celebrate that Americans are allowed to make contracts with other Americans regardless of sex. The just ruling by the Supreme Court reminds us of the liberty and religious liberties we given as citizens of this great country. Yet, the subtleties of law and what is necessary for a just society along with the difference in theological opinions are more complex than many want to spend time parsing. These rulings in the wider society also have the potential to create further division between those who hold differing views on marriage.

The Church (local, wider, and global) has suffered because of the belief that we should all agree on the matter of same-sex blessings and marriage; and that those who disagree should leave. This conflict of conscience has made it difficult for us to remain one church in a common mission. Our western culture of indictment teaches us to use power and force against those who do not agree with us. In a culture that is tied to outcomes with a winner and loser, we create communities of isolation in which we say good-bye to dear friends we disagree with and hide behind a sense of moral high ground. When the General Convention meeting in 2012 took action on rites for blessing same-sex relationships, issues of sexuality reignited at the diocesan and parish level—conflict had the potential to result in winners and losers. Through our work in the Diocese of Texas on *Unity and Mission* we were able to keep from creating great division, lawsuits costing millions of dollars, and pain that could have disrupted our ministry. Instead we ignited ministry; we continued to grow in both liberal and conservative congregations alike. We were able to be something different. We were able to stay together.

In a country of division on political and religious grounds we were able to bear witness that such division over differences is not a predetermined outcome. Staying together despite our deep theological divisions was and remains a witness to the Gospel's call for unity among the followers of Jesus.

Three years later, the issues facing us in the summer of 2015 once again threaten our focus on mission. I remain convinced that the igniting of anxiety, fear, and the culture wars are not a healthy response to difficult times. It is most assuredly not helpful for the purpose of mission and the proclamation of God in Christ Jesus. It is not a witness to reconciliation. We in the Episcopal Church are once again drawn into conflict and may seek to walk apart. Even as we are attempting to be faithful to our mission context our wider Anglican Church threatens to break apart under the weight of these disagreements.

Hope means having a realistic understanding of the past and present without nostalgia. As we look over our history as a diocese, and as we reflect on the history of our Church and the ancient scriptures that reach back to the very day that Abram set out from the land of Ur, we know that God's people have bickered with one another for ages. Scripture reminds us that such "quarreling over opinions" (Romans 14:1) is poor stewardship of our time and energy and does not serve our Lord well.

My gifts have typically been best used when mediating between differing parties. When we did the "walkabouts" in the diocese prior to my election as bishop, I explained that I would help us faithfully get through this theological, liturgical and cultural change. I knew that I had gifts to help us find a kind of unity that brings opposing groups to the table. I have been grateful for the leadership of so many who have joined me in calling for a unified witness to the Gospel and have given their time and energies to hold our church together—when the pressure to pull us apart was great.

After General Convention 2009, I knew I couldn't allow our Diocese of Texas to slip into division and conflict without action on my part. I approached former Secretary of State James Baker to help me think through the leadership that was required at this moment in history. I also began to read and think critically about my own position and what I thought was best for the Diocese. I returned to Secretary Baker to seek his guidance as we make our way through the time that is now before us in 2015. I have asked and prayed for clarity about how best to lead the Diocese of Texas. I have asked for wisdom about our witness and role to the wider Church and Anglican Communion. I took time on my sabbatical to review our *Unity and Mission* work. I also prayed about the divisions that we still face. I prayed about what I thought and tried to better understand my role in leadership as we face our future together—especially as it has to do with the divisive issues of sexuality and marriage.

I am grateful to Secretary Baker for his expertise and his guidance in what has become into a multiyear process of discernment and strategic thinking. I am especially grateful to him for his kind and stern words to me during a particularly rough patch of thinking and conversation. In November 2010, Secretary Baker took time for my phone call while in Washington, D.C., helping President Barack Obama get the START Treaty through Congress (which I think illustrates how important Secretary Baker

3 THE FUTURE WE CREATE

Over the last four decades The Episcopal Church has been in conflict with itself (on the Prayer Book, ordination of women and homosexuals, on blessing same-sex relationships, and marriage), while at the same time losing unparalleled numbers of members.

Statistics published in The Episcopal Church Annual of 2011 (p. 15) paint a bleak picture of changes between 2008 and 2009: 69 fewer parishes; 50,949 fewer baptized members; 42,177 fewer communicants in good standing; 22,294 fewer people in average Sunday attendance; 1,887 fewer baptisms; 597 fewer confirmations.

In 2010, the Diocese of Texas began to increase the number of baptisms and confirmations for the first time in more than a decade by focusing on mission and strategic growth. By 2014 we saw another growth in Average Sunday Attendance and we saw continued growth in membership. The Episcopal Church overall continues a greater decline. Even our progress on baptisms and confirmations does not make up for shrinking membership and Average Sunday Attendance.

We have a long way to go if we are to grow, and this growth will require new initiatives, new funding, and renewed focus. Building up a positive Episcopal identity, as unabashed Episcopalians and reclaiming the mission of the Church are essential ingredients. I refer here to my vision offered in *Unabashedly Episcopalian* and *Church: A Generous Community Amplified for the Future*. We must claim positively who we are and get back to work as God's Church undertaking God's mission.

There are certainly other cultural forces at work causing a decrease in attendance and we cannot blame the entire drop on the culture wars. Yet they are a very real factor. They are a factor for those who disagree with one another and they are a factor because the culture views our warring with one another as a failure towards peace—which is understood as a key ingredient of Christian life. Future growth is not possible in a Church at war with itself.

In the Diocese of Texas we are committed to planting new congregations and Christian communities. We have chosen to work together and stay together. The work to be done includes planting these new communities and improving our newcomer ministries to welcome people into our church and share with them the Gospel of Jesus Christ through the unique formation of Christians who are unabashedly Episcopalian. We also need to learn how to share the Gospel with people outside of our churches. We need to relearn the art and practice of being a neighbor to the community around us.

The Rev. Dr. Russell Levenson wrote an article in *The Living Church* that captured the reality of our decline with these words:

> *...the essential elements of decline began in the mid-1970s. In 1970, TEC had an all-time high of 3,475,164 members. Within five years, it had lost nearly half a million, down 3,039,136 (Episcopal Church Annual, p. 21). In the four decades since then, we bled out more than one-third of our members. Some will blame this drastic period of anemia on divisions over women's ordination, prayer book revision and even fallout from the civil rights movements of the 1960s, but it is probably not that simple either. A massive loss between 1970 and 1975 occurred before the height of divisions over women's ordination and prayer book revision.*[1]

Regarding the issues that have created conflict in the Episcopal Church, he writes:

> *Some will cite the 2003 General Convention, which approved the Episcopal Church's first openly gay bishop, as the turning point, and The Episcopal Church Annual again shows an important decline (see p. 21): we have lost more than 250,000 baptized members (from 2,284,233 to 2,006,343) and 325 parishes and missions (from 7,220 to 6,895). "Episcopal Congregations Overview" records that 89 percent of Episcopal congregations reported conflicts or disagreements in the last five years, and adds: "The ordination of gay priests or bishops was the most frequently mentioned source of conflict."*[2]

Both Dr. Levenson and the Very Rev. Joe Reynolds point out that the conflicts that stem from our differing views on sexuality are taking its toll on the church at large.

Over these four decades, The Episcopal Church has walked neither a merciful and loving way, nor a middle way. I believe we have approached the conversation, with a perspective of division on issues and not on unity in mission. There has been very little willingness by either side of the cultural/sexual issues for tolerance with one another. Each party has chosen to cast the other party out if there is no agreement.

In Paul Zahl's podcast Episode 53, entitled *How To Tell The Future*, he invites the listener to think about the science fiction author Philip Wylie's work and the reality that his predictions have been 90 percent accurate.[3] Zahl believes that Wylie's accuracy is due to the fact that Wylie holds two basic truths: 1) human nature does not change, 2) fashion and trends change. Zahl says these truths, when employed, will not create "friends in the present," but they will bring "awe in the future because of the accuracy" of our predictions.

When I was taking mediation courses at George Mason University and UT Law School, there was a perennial truth that was drilled into our psyches: when humans are in conflict, they move to a place of incapacity. In our natural and healthy reflective state we approach conflict feeling empowered to make decisions. We have the ability to consider other people's ideas. At this stage the conflict is simply a problem to be solved. As the conflict continues over time, we move gradually up the conflict scale. As we live in unresolved conflict, we begin to feel less power to make decisions and cannot tolerate another person's conflicting ideas. Conflicts at this stage are at a "fight or flight" stage. Our normal functioning becomes inactive when we feel the conflict consumes our lives. Here is a graph that shows what happens in conflict. The graph illustrates the reality that anxiety grows when people move from being able to listen to others and feeling empowered to solve problems to an intractable situation and a place of feeling powerless.

Self-absorbed/ Disempowered

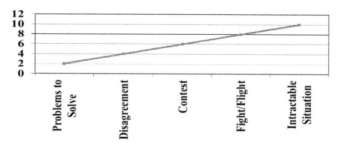

Other/E

mpowered

When we combine this information with Zahl's thesis that human nature does not change but, rather, only fashion changes, we are able to predict a future with accuracy.

As a Church we have approved the blessing of same-sex relationships. At General Convention 2015, the Church will have begun discernment on the marriage canons. This is in part due to the fact that state law is changing and in part due to the reality that clergy and laity alike are changing their understanding of marriage based upon their understanding of biology and scripture. Predictably, parts of the Church that have not been able to decrease the level of anxiety over the sexuality debate will succumb to a "fight or flight" condition.

While many dioceses have already moved past this point, there are still many dioceses in which the decisions from this Convention will cause an exodus. Churches still embroiled in this conflict will have their mission incapacitated by the conflict. Progressives in predominately traditional dioceses will continue to press for change and create conflict. Traditionalists will continue to fight over and against the leadership of TEC and against the liberals in their own dioceses. Such uses of time, energy, power and money drain resources that should be focused on, and used for, the proclamation of God in Christ Jesus.

While we have worked hard to respect our differences, I predict that human nature will overtake us and we will forget that our unity is in Christ and not in our forced agreement on sexuality issues and this will drive us into conflict once again. Despite all our efforts regarding *Unity and Mission*, sexuality continues to be a lightning rod for our anxiety and fear.

In another podcast entitled *Should I Stay or Should I Go?* Zahl challenges us to realize that we live in a culture of indictment.[4] We continue to live in a dualistic and conflicted culture in which "you are either with us or against us." We must stop being "against" one another and begin to be "for" Jesus. As our new Presiding Bishop-elect Michael Curry reminds us, "We are Jesus people!"

Our challenge is to move beyond the abysmal wreckage of these past four decades and say, "Enough is enough."

We must surmount the culture wars and return to the very real work of proclaiming a Gospel of mercy and love—in our hearts, in word and in deed. We must agree that we disagree—that this is a challenge to be faced and we must take action that will allow us to move forward into the mission field together.

In the Diocese of Texas we have faced challenges of division and conflict before and our bishops have led us through them intact. At the time of revolution when the earliest white Texians (as they were called) wrestled power from Mexico, our first missionary bishop, the Rt. Rev.

George Washington Freeman (who was appointed and paid for by the Episcopal Church Missionary Society) focused our attention on building up the Diocese of Texas. The seeds planted by his ministry and the support he gave our first clergy built a united company of faithful men and women who would petition and become the Episcopal Diocese of Texas. In the midst of settlement in the new state he argued for dollars to raise up missionaries.

During the Civil War, at a time when Texas was deeply divided, Bishop Alexander Gregg (our first diocesan bishop) focused on mission and the growth of congregations and schools throughout Texas. He was one of the first southern bishops to make his pledge to the Union after the war. The silver dollar he paid for his reinstatement was considered a collector's piece. While he could not attend the first General Convention of the Episcopal Church following the Civil War, he was one of the first bishops to lead his southern diocese back into union with the Episcopal Church. His commitment to keep us together in the midst of a divided Texas helped us to grow despite the culture war on slavery.

Bishop Gregg's witness and commitment to unity helped the people of the diocese envision hope for the future. We next elected a bridge builder, the Rt. Rev. George Herbert Kinsolving. He served on the Confederate side of the Civil War as a young man, yet was eager for reunification at its end. He was known as a low-church evangelical who was committed to unity even as his high-church brothers and sisters threatened to depart The Episcopal Church over the liturgical conflict that was dividing our Church at the time. Six-foot-six, he was known as *Texas George* and was an advocate for the freed men then seeking to build churches across the country and in Texas. His advocacy for black bishops to help oversee freedmen congregations was well known nationally. Upon his death he was mourned by the black leadership of The Episcopal Church across the country for his activism.

Bishop Clinton S. Quin, our third bishop, held an unmoving vision of a Gospel unleashed through evangelism, and he guided the expansion of Episcopal churches in Texas despite divisions brought about bad economies and war. A friend of the laity, he was able to hold the Diocese together and witness its growth during a time when the country struggled with two economic depressions and the First World War.

His successor, the Rt. Rev. John Hines, helped us live through the Civil Rights Era and later served as our Presiding Bishop. He endured the vitriol and hatred that infected our Councils at that time. Yet his prophetic witness—that the kingdom of God was a realm encompassing all people in an undivided society—he held the Diocese together. Despite the anger that threatened division and even disintegration of the Diocese of Texas under Hines' leadership, we continued to experience unprecedented growth in our churches and membership. Many parishioners recall this time to me and remind me that though we disagreed on the floor of our Diocesan Council we could be found together late into the evening in the company of brothers and sisters of the same Lord and Savior Jesus Christ.

The Rt. Rev. Milton Richardson succeeded Bishop Hines and was known for his wisdom and strength of leadership. Not only did he help guide us through the rest of the Civil Rights Era, but he also led us through the *Book of Common Prayer* revision and women's ordination. Bishop Richardson was the only bishop in the House of Bishops who voted against the 1979 *Book of Common Prayer*. Yet, after its approval by General Convention, he ushered in full use of the book, allowing for some congregations to maintain their use of the *1928 Book of Common Prayer*. We wrestled with women's ordination, but when he discerned it was time, he was present for the first ordination of a woman in the Diocese of Texas, the Rev. Helen Havens. And, when Texas itself raised up its first woman priest, he ordained the Rev. Elizabeth Masquelette. Bishop Richardson was thoroughly committed to The Episcopal Church. When parishioners were likely to complain about The Episcopal Church and challenge him not to send money, he would say, "You can't get all of the *New York Times* for a quarter." Even though he disagreed with the wider Church at times, being a full member of The Episcopal Church family was never in question.

The Rt. Rev. Maurice Benitez then helped us to more fully embrace women's ordination and brought greater liturgical innovation into the Diocese of Texas through the then-popular renewal movement. Things in the Diocese of Texas did change in this era, and we were bitterly divided on the issue of sexuality. Yet, we entered a period of time when institutions that were begun during previous bishops' tenures grew and took on new life. We began to plant new churches again. Bishop Benitez was certainly unhappy at times with the leadership of the wider Church, especially on the issue of sexuality, but he loved the Church and always spoke with passion about the Church in which he has stayed.

The election of the Rt. Rev. Claude E. Payne moved the Diocese to a more moderate but still traditional position. Bishop Payne, not unlike Bishop Richardson early in his tenure, did not feel it was time to deal with the issues that divided us. He urged and cheered the Diocese on to grow— to expect miraculous things of one another. He held a traditionalist stance, but he did not let the culture wars distract us from mission and the Gospel of Jesus Christ.

In 2003, the Rt. Rev. Don A. Wimberly brought sound leadership to the

4 THE RESPONSIBILITY OF BISHOP AS LEADER

When confronting change I am often challenged to explain my reasons for making the change. Why not simply allow change to come to us? Or, why not disregard the changes around same-sex blessings or marriage completely? The chief of these reasons is that I am called as a bishop to uphold two opposing forces: unity and tradition. I am to be a leader, even if that means leading in ways that are different from how people would prefer. This is the responsibility of every bishop.

As bishop I intend to lead through the current crisis that faces us in the Diocese of Texas, our Episcopal Church, and the wider Anglican Communion. I believe I am leading out of a tradition of bold Texas bishops, and I also have clarity in my vocation as bishop. I am a bishop of the Diocese of Texas, a bishop of the Episcopal Church and a bishop within the Anglican Communion. This is my work as a leader. My guess is that you are most likely given a different role to play; however, in order to read this text from my perspective it seems necessary here to pause and think a bit about the role I, and all bishops play in our current historical moment.

For me, the task is to be faithful to the faith I have received and the call of God on my heart to do the work of God's mission of reconciliation that is set before me. I believe that above all else I am a bishop of the Church of God. In my ordination I testified that I would uphold the doctrine and discipline of the Church as I have received them, and that I am so persuaded of my call to be bishop that I am willing, regardless of cost, to carry out the vocation I have inherited faithfully and diligently. Moreover, I understand I am to bring about (with the clergy and laity of my diocese) a healthy growing church—a missionary church—and, at day's end, am to leave the Church alive and well for those who follow. I have a legacy of delivering a unified and missionary church.

Jesus Christ is our great high priest. The outward flowing of the inner life of God, which we know as Trinity, is revealed and manifested in Baptism and Eucharist. In our Anglican and Episcopal tradition I am chief president and primary sacramentalist for the Episcopal community in which I am called to serve. I am the chief liturgist—I am responsible for ordering our common life of ministry to enable order and communion between all of our many and diverse parts. A document produced by and published by the Inter-Anglican Doctrinal Commission, in October of 2007, entitled *The Anglican Way: The Significance of the Episcopal Office for the Communion of the Church* [TSEO] says that as bishop I am the "focal person who links parishes within a diocese not only to one another but also the diocese to the wider Church within the Communion and ecumenically."[5] We might also remember that this echoes our own Episcopal ordination service, which says that I am ordained as bishop to "wisely oversee the life and work of the church."[6] At once, my vocation and my office are both contextually and universally catholic.

The unique proclamation of the Good News of Salvation through Jesus Christ is my particular evangelical office. Bishop Payne used to say, "The bishop is the chief evangelist." It is my work to give voice to the mission of God's people and their community, the Church. It is my work to share the practice and proclamation of the Good News as it is exemplified in the many and diverse communities throughout the Diocese, the wider Episcopal Church, and Communion. I believe it is my work to make Jesus known in each community that I visit, to help each to see Christ in their midst. Moreover, my work is to take with me the particular representation of the incarnate Christ discovered and to represent that to the next congregation I visit. The role of narrating the miraculous reconciling work of Jesus Christ locally is a role that invites me to speak prophetically to the Church and its people. It is my daily work of devotion, study and reflection that prepares me to "know Christ, to know the power of his resurrection; and to enter into the fellowship of sharing his sufferings."[7] It is my evangelical work to make Christ known in the Church and beyond.

Within one week in August 2011, I visited a small congregation in the lower Shire valley in Southern Malawi and then a small congregation in Freeport, Texas. Both congregations gave voice to the notion that I, as bishop, had incarnated the global communion to them. Both congregations were aware of the work of Christ in their midst and far away in a distant country. In this one week, people living on opposite sides of the globe were truly and effectively one and bore witness to both the prophetic voice of unity and mission that I carried. Both were bound together through the apostolic witness of a universal church and fellowship.

I want to spend my life encouraging believers into this one body of faith, deeply rooted in our apostolic heritage. It is my vocation to guard the faith and to help Christ build up the faith. It is a faith heritage of "patriarchs, prophets, apostles, and martyrs and those of every generation."[8] It is my responsibility to hold fast to the teachings of the apostolic Church through time and space, symbolized by my own apostolic succession. It is my work to witness to the faith once delivered to the saints and to preserve a living orthodoxy: worship, believing and practice.

We cannot use dogma, which we believe is essential, to bludgeon our fellow Christians or those who seek a living Christ. We must be faithful to the Gospel, but we cannot condemn the mission field we wish to convert or condemn one another. We might do well to remember that Jesus did not come to condemn the world. We can easily bring to mind the words of John 3.16: "For God so loved the world that he gave his only Son, so that everyone who believes in him may not perish but may have eternal life." We often forget Jesus' next words: "Indeed, God did not send the Son into the world to condemn the world, but in order that the world might be saved through him." Another passage that challenges us is John 7:53-8:11 in which Jesus deals with the adulterous woman. In this passage Jesus turns his living word into action, enacting John 3:17 in his conversation with this woman. Lifting up the woman from the ground, Jesus says to her, "Has no one condemned you?" She said, "No one, sir." And Jesus said, "Neither do I condemn you." It is my vocation, like the ministry of Jesus, to be "merciful to all, show compassion to the poor and strangers, and defend those who have no helper."[9] I am to come to the aid of the condemned and the condemner alike.

In order to live life in the Church with one another, we must be careful to discern the essentials and the nonessentials. While we have not done this very well over the last four decades, it is our vocation to do so now. I pray for courage and wisdom in the undertaking of this vocation for I am responsible for praying the Holy Spirit into the ancient teachings once received in order that the true faith of the Gospel of Jesus Christ might flourish.[10]

As Brian McLaren recently wrote, beneath our stated belief is every person's deeply "cherished experience of God and nearness to God."[11] I endeavor therefore to raise faithful followers of Jesus Christ who rest upon our theological legacy of scripture, tradition and reason and who are animated because of their heart experience of God. It is my work to build a scripture-formed people for God.

There is no diocese without a bishop and the reverse is true. The bishop is always in a particular context but also in the midst of a particular people.

It is my vocation to work with the people and specifically with the baptized. It is the work of the bishop to order and coordinate the gifts of the Church for the mission of the Christ. We understand that the gifts of the baptized are not the property of any one person but are given to each to edify the body of Christ, his Church, for the purpose of serving God and his mission. "We are all members one of another," writes Paul in his letter to the Romans (12:5). The idea that we are all genuinely family, and that together we are a strong missionary community, is deeply rooted in our Diocese of Texas history. We have been a diocese with a history of strong bishops who brought many gifts, but we also know the names of the clergy and lay people who stood next to them and helped to build the mission of the Church with their immense generosity and stewardship.

One of the special ministries that I have as bishop is my relationship with my clergy. Our clergy share with me in carrying out the mission of the Church. I have a vocation to pastorally and spiritually provide an environment in which they may grow and flourish in the freedom of the Holy Spirit. Together we must engage in the work that is before us, deeply grounded in an exchange of prayer and scripture. This result is a shared sense of ministry where we all undertake the work of liturgy, proclamation and formation together. Therefore, I feel responsible to come to the aid of clergy under my care, offer resources to help each respond to their local context, and to lead through the conflict that may arise following General Convention.

Today, some people of the Diocese of Texas are faced with a great conflict of conscience. It is an anthropological conflict and it is a conflict on the theology and liturgy of marriage. It is a conflict on the nature of human sexuality. It is a conflict that we have been debating at Diocesan Council since the late eighties, but it is deeply rooted in unsettled conflict around divorce and so we may see that the nativity of our current debate on the nature of marriage predates most of our own births.

It is my vocation as bishop to "recall the broken and conflicted body of Christ to its reconciled life in him."[12] My vocation of mediating disputes within the family of God is normally a work undertaken on a congregational level and within a much more confined context..

We believe, and we proclaim in our mission and vision statement of the Diocese of Texas, that we are "reconciled by Christ" and that we value our unity. Is this not the work of the church—reconciliation? Our work is to heal history. It is to live with difference and celebrate our breadth or catholicity. It is to create a commons of peace where all can gather around the table.[13] In our conflict on marriage and sexuality we are currently not reconciled one to another, yet we prize unity as a goal. Even though we are bone-weary from the fight, we have soldiered on in conflict and have so sought our own will, that we have been willing to divide the body of Christ itself. We have been willing to indict one another based upon our assurance of right, forgetting we are to imitate Jesus' ministry and mission of mercy and love, and forgetting Peter and Paul's commitment to unity over division.

While this is our current reality, I am challenged by the text from TSEO where we find these words, "Most obviously the Church is made up of frail and foolish people. The upward call of Christ presumes we are sinners in need of God's grace, forgiveness and mercy. In this context, *koinonia* (the intimate communion of God) is necessarily a partial and vulnerable reality. A bishop's vocation involves tending this *koinonia* through the wise handling of conflict. The challenge for bishops is how to harness conflicts so that through this process a deeper *koinonia* in the Gospel emerges."[14] This is a call to ministry that I am willing to answer as bishop diocesan.

It is my vocation to help us, as a diocese, deal with the issues that feed our division and keep us from the work of the Gospel, and to help us do so in a manner that helps each of us engage God and Jesus Christ in a deeper manner—drinking deeply from the spiritual waters that heal and restore the creatures of God.

Another vocational aspect of my Episcopal life regarding this conflict is my role to connect the baptized people of God across every boundary—to make catholic what is experienced as diversity. Diversity is not a core value of our faith—catholicity is. We have a confidence in a tradition of apostolic faith that is expressed and proclaimed in a variety of missionary contexts. The unique story of the gift of Jesus Christ, our Trinitarian faith, our doctrine and our worship are shared in every context. I understand that my office and ministry personify this catholic, universal temperament of the Gospel. Being in communion with other bishops is an essential part of this ministry because it incarnates the unifying reality of Christ throughout the world. Being in communion with completely dissimilar parishes is another example of this unifying catholicity in the midst of a varied diocese and larger Church.

I turn here again to the text from TSEO. I believe it so clearly articulates the vocation of catholicity: The catholicity of the [episcopal] office means the bishop is an agent of the fullness of the one faith expressed through myriad local forms.[15]

Our Anglican and Episcopal faith has historically understood and practiced a polity in which our catholicity is always connected to our context and our local culture through the bishop. This can be a challenge. Therefore, in our model of church this connection to culture and the context places the bishop in a special ministry of translating locally what is received from abroad and translating abroad what is received locally. The bishop then becomes an icon of both the local and global expressions of church. The commission continues:

> *Enculturation that is authentic plumbs the heart of the Christian faith. This requires active engagement with the local cultures so that any stumbling blocks to the hearing, receiving and enacting of the gospel be removed. When this occurs the gifts of the people are harnessed for authentic mission in that time and place. A bishop must truly know the local cultures and values of the people that the bishop has been called to serve and lead. This can be a real challenge, for the bishop is chief pastor within and across particular ethnic, racial, and cultural contexts. Yet in this role the bishop has to ensure that the one catholic faith finds expression through these particular identities without becoming subsumed by them. The catholicity of the office requires a way of life that is constantly in dialogue with others (especially including other bishops) across many boundaries.[16]*

As a bishop, I am always aware that I serve a wider faith body. I am always at once bishop of Texas, bishop in The Episcopal Church, and bishop in the Anglican Communion. In the same way I am a witness to our catholicity of our local expression of church to the wider province and communion.

> *Catholicity also means that the decisions that come from any local place are not simply "local" decisions, but affect all. Bishops have a particular responsibility to bring the Church catholic into local processes of discerning the apostolic faith. They also have a responsibility to represent their diocese to the rest of the Church, to interpret to the Communion the realities of their local place. This means explaining not simply the end results of decisions reached, but being able to give theological explanation of the discernment of the gospel in the culture, and of the catholicity of such decisions. Bishops need the courage and wisdom to be able to hear the voice of others, whether within or outside their contexts.[17]*

It is my particular vocation to bring the broadest global view into our dialog and discernment on all matters of church, and to represent the diversity of voices; and to represent our dialog globally to make catholic a church family, a diocesan family, which consists of people from different cultures, class, sex, race and different views of marriage and sexuality. I am also responsible for communicating our particular context in Texas to the rest of the Church so that bonds of affection may grow despite the stumbling blocks a diversity of opinion may bring. I am at once a bishop in

God's Holy Church and at the same time shepherd of "[my] people."[18] Every bishop is tasked with this work of guarding the unity and yet articulating our catholicity and difference, which is a God-given gift, into their present context.

We hide from our catholicity with words like *conservatives* or *traditionalists* and *liberals* or *progressives*. However, to break up the discourse into two camps is to have failed already. We are one family, which is nothing less than the family of God, and within that family are various and divergent individual voices. We are intimately connected with individuals throughout our community and world. In our family we have sons and daughters, parents and grandparents, clergy and laity, who seek to help decipher the Church's teachings, and more importantly who need help to reconcile their firm feelings about the closeness of God and the sense that the Church cares for them.

Finally and perhaps ultimately, it is my vocation to be and participate in the wider community of bishops where I seek to maintain a healthy bond with my fellow bishops. My work and actions are never lived out in a vacuum. I share a life of ministry with my fellow bishops[19] and how I lead locally impacts them.

It is my vocation to be chief liturgist, evangelist, apostolic teacher and binder of our faith, a partner with clergy and laity alike, a mediator of God's grace, an encourager of reconciliation, catholic, and a colleague with my brother and sister bishops. My episcopal life, prayer and discernment have taught me that if I endeavor to lead or do anything without these vocations in the forefront of my mind I am being unfaithful to God's calling.

I am supported by nearly 200 years of the historical witness of our Diocese of Texas bishops who have, against great odds and tumultuous division, maintained the unity of Christ's mission and have forged a great diocese despite periodic fires of disunion.

It is then in the great tradition of our Texas bishops and out of my own understanding of the vocation and office of bishop that I come to bring my attention to the matter of our unity in mission above and beyond the cultural wars, and division on marriage and sexuality. I make my stand defending the catholic and reformed faith that is in me with sound reasoning and great charity in order that the mission of the Good News of salvation and our proclamation of the uniqueness of God in Christ Jesus might be sustained. I am therefore committed to unity not for the sake of compromise and peace but as a means of comprehension and truth.[20] I make my stand for the mission of the Gospel "that the world may believe." (John 20:20)

5 UNITY AS AN INSTRUMENT OF MISSION

As a bishop I often have the pleasure of hearing the blessed Samuel John Stone's 1868 hymn "The Church's One Foundation." While it was written following the Civil War and the reuniting of our Episcopal Church, it was, in fact, written for a very different reason. In 1866, an influential and liberal Anglican bishop wrote a book that attacked the historic accuracy of the Pentateuch. This caused a widespread controversy throughout the Anglican Church. Samuel John Stone, a pastor ministering to the poor of London at the time, was deeply upset by the schism that surrounded him. He wrote a collection of 12 creedal hymns. He understood, above all things, that the foundation of the Church must be the Lordship of Christ and not the views of any one group of people. His hymn "The Church's One Foundation" was based on the Ninth Article of the Apostles' Creed. In his time it read: "The Holy Catholic (or Universal) Church; the Communion of Saints; He is the head of this Body." These are words today that always move me and remind me of the awesome work we in the Church choose to undertake, and upon whom we depend most of all.

The Church's one foundation is Jesus Christ her Lord;
she is his new creation,
by water and the word:
from heaven he came and sought her to be his holy bride;
with his own blood he bought her, and for her life he died.
Elect from every nation,
yet one o'er all the earth,
her charter of salvation,
one Lord, one faith, one birth;
one holy Name she blesses,
partakes one holy food,

and to one hope she presses,
with every grace endued.
Though with a scornful wonder men see her sore oppressed,
by schisms rent asunder,
by heresies distressed;
yet saints their watch are keeping, their cry goes up,
"How long?" and soon the night of weeping shall be
the morn of song.
Mid toil and tribulation, and tumult of her war
she waits the consummation of peace for evermore;
till with the vision glorious
her longing eyes are blessed, and the great Church victorious
shall be the Church at rest.
Yet she on earth hath union with God, the Three in one,
and mystic sweet communion with those whose rest is won.
O happy ones and holy!
Lord, give us grace that we like them, the meek and lowly,
on high may dwell with thee.[21]

We seek to live these words despite our disagreements, our desire to have our own way, and our sinful want to fight rather than to engage in mission.

Our own efforts for unity depend partially on each of us, but only in a limited way. Paul's letter to the Philippians, Chapter 2, offers us these words on unity for the sake of mission.

If then there is any encouragement in Christ, any consolation from love, any sharing in the Spirit, any compassion and sympathy, make my joy complete: be of the same mind, having the same love, being in full accord and of one mind. Do nothing from selfish ambition or conceit, but in humility regard others as better than yourselves. Let each of you look not to your own interests, but to the interests of others. Let the same mind be in you that was in Christ Jesus, who, though he was in the form of God, did not regard equality with God as something to be exploited, but emptied himself, taking the form of a slave, being born in human likeness. And being found in human form, he humbled himself and became obedient to the point of death— even death on a cross. Therefore God also highly exalted him and gave him the name that is above every name, so that at the name of Jesus every knee should bend, in heaven and on earth and under the earth, and every tongue should confess that Jesus Christ is Lord, to the glory of God the Father.

We are called by God to be "in full accord and one mind" for the sake of the Gospel of Jesus Christ. We cannot begin to offer a strategy on how best to proceed through the conflict that is upon us if we do not proceed in common mission under the headship of Jesus Christ. Effective mission hinges on the unity of the Church. This unity is so essential that before his death, Jesus prays for us asking God to make us one. He prays for his disciples and for us saying, "May they become completely one, so that the world may know that you have sent me."[21]

Throughout his ministry, St. Paul pleaded with the Church to "be in agreement." Let there be "no divisions among you. Be united in the same mind and same purpose," he wrote in his first letter to the Corinthians (1:10). Yet, the first Christians were deeply divided over many different things. They were divided because the mission to the Jews and the mission to the Gentiles were in conflict. The early Christian community inherited religious practices from the Jewish tradition that were icons and sacramental ways of life and were in direct conflict with the Gentile way of life. Much of the Book of Acts and Paul's letters are filled with descriptions of how the early church dealt with what was essentially a conflict created by two colliding cultures. Specifically, we might recall Paul's thoughts on the morality of eating meat offered to idols. In fact, two of Paul's letters addressed this particular pastoral issue because it was so divisive to this growing Christian community. Rather than appealing to the law, Paul reminded believers of the freedom they have in Christ. Christians, Paul insisted, are free to follow their conscience and are free from the burden of judging or changing others. Christians are not only free from but prohibited from indicting and sentencing those who are different because of the freedom we have in Christ Jesus.[22]

"Who are you," Paul asked, "to pass judgment on servants of another? It is before their own lord that they stand or fall. Let all be fully convinced in their own minds. The faith you have, have as your own conviction before God."[23] How can a Church so deeply divided over the morality of this issue still "be in agreement?"[24] The first Christians embraced the Gospel truth that Christ is our unity. What glues the Church together is "the message of the cross," Paul wrote. Our diverse yet faithfully held positions shall in the end be laid at the altar of God. Until that time our faith in Jesus Christ unites us and draws us into the mission field.

In this we find a manner of living with one another in a covenant community. If we imitate Christ and his manner, we too will find unity in our faith and in our work. Paul's words challenge us to be unified for mission some two thousand years later.

Paul challenges us: "Do not look to your own interests, but to the interests of others. Let the same mind be in you that was in Christ Jesus, who, though he was in the form of God, did not regard equality with God as something to be exploited." Though we are members of the Abrahamic faith, the family of God, we are not to exploit or use it to our own benefit. We are not to use our partnership with God as a means to judge and condemn others. We are to act with mercy, forgiveness, love and kindness. This work of mercy is so difficult that, like Jesus, we must empty ourselves in order to be filled with grace. Today the world tells us to fill up ourselves, to consume, to be served, to attach ourselves to others, to over-identify ourselves with others. Detachment is an ancient Christian practice, though in our current culture we attach and over-identify with others. We are a culture that consumes and we consume one another and consume ourselves. Listen to St. Paul's words, "[Be like Jesus who] emptied himself, taking the form of a slave." This is a radical way of being with one another.

In our conflicts we spend so much time attempting the destruction of one another that there is nothing left in the person or in the relationship to be served. From the beginning of Genesis, chapter 1, we are reminded of our long history of blaming others. Adam blames Eve and Eve blames the snake. This scripture reminds us of our fallen nature and how easy it is to scapegoat others rather than owning our own responsibility. We, by our fallen nature, find it enticing to have an enemy we can consume rather than the brother or sister God invites us to make family. Our Gospel challenges us, through the blessings of grace received, to empty ourselves and our natural desires to judge and condemn, so that we can come alongside our fellow Christian with the love, mercy and forgiveness of Jesus.

This is the unifying mind of Christ. It is a unity that understands hospitality and love and is obedient, no matter how abusive someone else might get. You and I are challenged by the reconciling love of Jesus Christ to be different from the world around us.

After meeting all day, a few bishops gathered late one evening to talk about and solve the problems of the world. One bishop got really angry and said the "other side" deserves what they get because they were so hostile to the minority long ago. I challenged him (and myself). I said that the task of the Christian is not to require an eye for an eye, but to be a witness of grace and mercy, no matter what is given. In return the Christian empties the natural desire to harm in order to have the mind of Christ, which is to love.

When ideological opponents in the Church can cease judgment of one another and serve one another, only then is the mission of Christ successful. When we have the mind of Christ and act with mercy, grace, love and kindness, then the kingdom of God is revealed before us.

I have lunch with a mentor and friend on a regular basis. He has been caught up in the culture wars that have infected the church, yet he is a man of incredible love, mercy and kindness. He challenged me to explain how we know what unifies us if we are not unified on our understanding of sexuality and on the issue of marriage or same-sex relationships. He, of course, knew well what the answer was. I believe he also knew that the culture wars have created a great lie within the Church--that if we are not unified on the issues of sexuality, then we must not be unified at all.

The reality is what the scripture tells us, and what Paul and Peter specifically tried to convey to the earliest Church. When one leaves, moves away or chooses to live outside of the community of God as we have received it in the one, holy, catholic, and apostolic fashion, they move away from God.

The rector for whom I first worked once looked me in the eye and said, "Andy, God will not bless division and conflict. It is not God's way." I think he is marvelously correct. When we turn inward and fight among ourselves, God does not bless our efforts, and the fruits of our labor rot upon the tree. In fact, there is much that unifies us as members of our Anglican and Episcopal Church.

Common Marks of Anglican Tradition

There are, in fact, very real marks of our Anglican tradition throughout our life as Church. These marks are common to us here in the Diocese of Texas just as they are common to the Church across the world. These marks are the particular icons of how we live out our lives as Christians. They are marks of our unique expression of the Anglican way of being the One, Holy, Catholic and Apostolic Church of Jesus Christ.[25] The Anglican Primates' Commission on Education [TEAC] noted the following marks are found in churches throughout the Anglican Communion: "Churches are formed by and rooted in scripture, shaped by its worship of the living God, ordered for communion, and directed in faithfulness to God's mission in the world."[26] They continue with this statement, "In diverse global situations Anglican life and ministry witnesses to the incarnate, crucified and risen Lord, and is empowered by the Holy Spirit. Together with all Christians, Anglicans hope, pray and work for the coming of the reign of God."[27]

We see that this echoes our own Episcopal understanding of the Christian hope, which is a life lived bearing witness to Christ, using our gifts to continue his work, and carrying out the work of reconciliation.[28] Episcopalians, like all Anglicans, are formed by the reading and studying of scripture.[29] TEAC produced this statement describing this essential DNA of our tradition:

> *As Anglicans we discern the voice of the living God in the Holy Scriptures, mediated by tradition and reason. We read the Bible together, corporately and individually, with a grateful and critical sense of the past, a vigorous engagement with the present, and with patient hope for God's future.*
>
> *We cherish the whole of Scripture for every aspect of our lives, and we value the many ways in which it teaches us to follow Christ faithfully in a variety of contexts. We pray and sing the Scriptures through liturgy and hymnody. Lectionaries connect us with the breadth of the Bible, and through preaching we interpret and apply the fullness of Scripture to our shared life in the world.[30]*

The Windsor Report recognizes that our attachment to scripture grew out of the "early Anglican reformers on the importance of the Bible and the Fathers over and against what they saw as illegitimate medieval developments. It was part of their appeal to ancient undivided Christian faith and life."[31] The seventeenth- and eighteenth-century theologians (called "divines") hammered out their foundations of scripture, tradition and reason. Scripture was always the most important element. Nineteenth-century theologians produced The Chicago-Lambeth Quadrilateral. It, too, echoes the Anglican Communion's notion that scripture is the foundation of theological discourse.[32] The Baptismal Covenant, Ordination Rites and the Catechism are all documents that reflect that The Episcopal Church still considers scripture as a common binding element of our Anglican faith.[33]

The people and the churches of the Diocese of Texas reflect this key and essential mark of Anglicanism. Regardless of which congregation I visit, I am assured to find people engaged in reading the scriptures. Our calendars are filled with Bible studies for almost every age. Some are led by clergy, but many more are led by laity. Still more present are the Bible studies that come before meetings in order to ensure that decision-making is born out of an engagement with scripture. Scriptural texts fill our prayer books and hymnals. The authors of the Windsor Report write:

> *This means that for scripture to "work" as the vehicle of God's authority it is vital that it be read at the heart of worship in a way which (through appropriate lectionaries, and the use of scripture in canticles, etc.) allows it to be heard, understood and reflected upon, not as a pleasing and religious background noise, but as God's living and active word. The message of scripture, as a whole and in its several parts, must be preached and taught in all possible and appropriate ways.[34]*

Scripture is the basis of the rich tradition of inherited historical documents, many of which are provided in the back of our *Book of Common Prayer*.[35] The importance of scripture has long been a foundation for our churches' decision-making. TEAC wrote this about how scripture has permeated our decision making: "They have shaped our rich inheritance: for example, the ecumenical creeds of the early Church, the *Book of Common Prayer*, and Anglican formularies such as the Articles of Religion, catechisms, and the Lambeth Quadrilateral."[36]

Anglicans, unlike many other Christians, have not only enjoyed a long and enduring love affair with scripture, but they have continuously engaged in studying it. We have a collect that reminds us of the importance of the scripture to us. It calls us to read, mark and inwardly digest the scriptures. As Anglicans, we are not afraid to engage scripture as a "true learning community."[37]

The fact that we read our texts with a scholarly eye, and have always done so, highlights one of the important aspects of who we are as Anglicans and Episcopalians. We understand that we read the biblical texts within a given community. We are reading the scripture in the midst of a living community, which is in turn engaging the Bible and the world around it. This means that we look to the scholar, the disciple, and the members of our community to help us interpret and engage the scripture. We are not afraid of the challenge of listening to others and their interpretation. The TEAC reports said it this way: "We desire to be a true learning community as we live out our faith, looking to one another for wisdom, strength and hope on our journey. We constantly discover that new situations call for fresh expressions of a scripturally informed faith and spiritual life."[38]

Alan Bartlett in *A Passionate Balance: The Anglican Tradition* wrote this story showing the complexity and length to which Anglicans will go to engage deeply the scripture that is before them:

A gifted Nigerian priest was studying at a college in the north of England. He was writing a thesis on the household codes at the end of the Pauline Epistles. He was especially looking at the teaching about the roles of men and women in the marriage and family. He finished his study by telling us that, in his context, if this teaching was adopted it would radically improve the treatment of women. But then he asked a wider question about how we were to understand the purpose of these texts? Were they intended to provide a law for all time....or were they, especially in the light of the life and teaching of Jesus, to be seen as contextual and instrumental pieces of teaching by Paul? Their purpose was precisely to improve the treatment of women by men in these Christian communities at that time, but....this teaching sat on top of a much bigger biblical trajectory, which was about the flourishing of women (and men) in God and that trajectory had a much more radical and open-ended agenda.[39]

Another wonderful quote comes from the writer Eugene Peterson:

Reading scripture constitutes an act of crisis. Day after day, week after week, it brings us into a world that is totally at odds with the type of world that newspaper and television serve up to us on a platter as our daily ration of data for conversation and concern. It is a world where God is active everywhere and always, where God is fiery first cause and not occasional afterthought, where God cannot be procrastinated, where everything is relative to God and God is not relative to anything. Reading scripture involves a dizzying reorientation of our culture-condition and job-oriented assumptions.[40]

Scripture is so central to our identity as Anglicans that it is considered the first bond of communion. The Windsor Report places scripture and its study at the center of our unity.[41] It is the Church's supreme authority.

At the same time as we claim this as an essential bond and common mark of our communion, the common phrase "'the authority of scripture' can be misleading; the confusions that result may relate to some of the divisions just noted."[42] This is a very complicated notion and so I want to quote directly from the Windsor Report here:

Scripture itself, after all, regularly speaks of God as the supreme authority. When Jesus speaks of "all authority in heaven and earth" (Matthew 28.18), he declares that this authority is given, not to the books that his followers will write, but to himself. Jesus, the living Word, is the one to whom the written Word bears witness as God's ultimate and personal self-expression. The New Testament is full of similar ascriptions of authority to the Father, to Jesus Christ, and to the Holy Spirit. Thus the phrase "the authority of scripture," if it is to be based on what scripture itself says, must be regarded as a shorthand, and a potentially misleading one at that, for the longer and more complex notion of "the authority of the triune God, exercised through scripture."[43]

It is this understanding that keeps Anglicans and Episcopalians from becoming narrow in their reading of the text. Take, for instance, the reading of the text by the Nigerian priest understanding the contextual reading of new freedoms for women in Nigeria. The same reading would appear to be oppressive in a more Western context. Therefore, as many scholars point out, taking a text and applying it universally as to meaning and practice can prove problematic in context.

The scripture is always pointing to the revelation of who God is. The early Christian Church was challenged to interpret God's revelation through the ancient Hebrew texts to a changed context, just as we read the text within an ever-changing community and are challenged by our context of mission today.

The authors of the Windsor Report help us understand how this Anglican form of reading scripture has created (between text and context) a dynamic, revelatory practice. As Anglicans, we see and understand that whether at a vestry meeting, women's meeting, youth event, or Bible study the revelation of God and Jesus Christ through the power of the Holy Spirit is a continuous breaking into our world and reality.

Again our authors of the Windsor Report help us to understand how Anglicans comprehend that the Holy Spirit breathes into our lives and vocations through the reading of scripture.

> *For Jesus and the early Christians, "authority" was not conceived as a static source of information or the giving of orders (as the word "authority" has sometimes implied), but in terms of the dynamic in breaking of God's kingdom, that is, God's sovereign, saving, redeeming and reconciling rule over all creation. This saving rule of God, long promised and awaited in Israel, broke in upon the world in and through Jesus and his death and resurrection, to be then implemented through the work of the Spirit until the final act of grace which will create the promised new heavens and new earth. If the notion of scriptural authority is itself to be rooted in scripture, and to be consonant with the central truths confessed by Christians from the earliest days, it must be seen that the purpose of scripture is not simply to supply true information, nor just to prescribe in matters of belief and conduct, nor merely to act as a court of appeal, but to be part of the dynamic life of the Spirit through which God the Father is making the victory which was won by Jesus' death and resurrection operative within the world and in and through human beings."*[44]

Our responsibility is to engage scripture. We are to work together so that "each individual Christian, to the fullest extent of which they are capable, must study it and learn from it, thoughtfully and prayerfully."[45] As clergy and lay leaders, we have an obligation to lay a fertile ground in which our Church can grow into a developed faith through the study of scripture.[46]

In the Episcopal Church, through our *Book of Common Prayer*, and specifically in the Baptismal Covenant, we proclaim that we will continue in the "apostles' teaching."[47] Our Episcopal tradition tells us that the scriptures are the Word of God, the Holy Spirit still speaks to us, and we read them that we may understand the life and teachings of Jesus.[48] We believe the Holy Spirit guides us in a "true interpretation."[49]

As a unique part of the Episcopal tradition, we publicly make our vow to God and before one another that we will seek God through the scriptures. We understand, and speak out loud, that an important part of the role of living life as church is the scripture. Scripture reinforces our unity in Christ. It is in scripture that the church is described as the body, with Christ as its head. Saint Paul wrote, "And God placed all things under his feet and appointed him to be head over everything for the church, which is his body, the fullness of him who fills everything in every way." (Ephesians 1:22ff)

In the Episcopal Church we stand and make our witness that scripture is an essential guidepost for being Anglicans/Episcopalians who choose to follow Jesus and Lord and Savior. Our particular and unique way of using scripture throughout our worship, our critical study as prerequisites to our theology, and our understanding that the Holy Spirit is always moving us to see Christ in our mission context are unique marks of our Christian life. It is from scripture that we find the revelation of our potential life in Christ, our unity, and our mission.

Shaped through Worship

The second mark of our unity as Anglicans is our worship. When I visit with new members, they often tell me it is our worship that draws them into community. Our worship, regardless of its contextual face, is life-giving.

Our tradition of Anglican worship has always bound us together. Authors of the English Reformation speak of a unified church despite differences. For instance, "It is not necessary that Traditions and Ceremonies be in all places one, or utterly like; for at all times they have been diverse..."[50]

It has been true for the Anglican Church ever since, and the breadth and commonality of our worship and common prayer bind us still, despite our differences on many issues.

Over the centuries the importance of our worship as a mission tool engaging with the culture has played a central role in the health and vitality of our Communion's mission. Moreover, our experience of shared worship (especially through Baptism and the Eucharist) is unifying in and of itself.

When I have traveled to Mexico, England, Southern Malawi, Central Ecuador, and when I travel to the many congregations of our Diocese, I can promise you that it is the continuum of our prayer and the traditional flow of scripture, hymnody, proclamation, forgiveness, table fellowship, and dismissal into the missionary field that fills my heart with the notion that I am a bishop of a unified diocese unified in Christ despite the diverse opinions on sexuality. Moreover, as Texas bishops before me, I enjoy the health and vitality of relationships globally.

We might remember well the words of St. Augustine in his confessions (4th century), which remind us of our ever seeking and imperfect vision of God's glory. For Augustine lived in a time when there were many Christian liturgies within a Catholic church. He writes:

> Can any praise be worthy of the Lord's majesty? How magnificent is his strength! How inscrutable his wisdom! We are one of your creatures, Lord, and our instinct is to praise you. We bear about us the mark of death, the sign of our own sin, to remind us that you thwart the proud. But still, since we are part of your creation, we wish to praise you. The thought of you stirs us so deeply that we cannot be content unless we praise you, because you made us for yourself and our hearts are restless until they find their rest in you.[51]

Our common worship in the Anglican and Episcopal tradition is a shared road map upon which we make our pilgrim journey to God in a common manner. We seek in all things, and especially in worship, to glorify God. The TEAC document that I referred to earlier makes this statement about how we share common Anglican traits regarding our liturgy:

> In the Anglican tradition particular importance is given to worship together in common as the gathered people of God. A life-long Anglican comments, "You give thanks all day long, but giving thanks together must be part of that thanksgiving." As we gather for worship we bring with us the joys and sorrows of our varied everyday lives. When we open ourselves to God in worship, our eyes are opened to God's ways with the world and we are empowered for service and mission.
>
> ...This means that our shared worship is vital for our life together as Christian disciples.[52]

Our formation and transformation are tied more directly to God in worship. Our common life in context (from coast to coast, from country to country) is intertwined in worship. The Holy Spirit is at work in our worship to bind us together. Our individual and corporate connection with God is cultivated. We "unite ourselves with others to acknowledge the holiness of God, to hear God's word, to offer prayer, and to celebrate the sacraments."[53] In part, we experience in worship the very real presence of God the creator, God who is incarnate and works salvation in the world,

God who is the spirit of love challenging us towards greater unity, and a God who invites us to join him as partners in building up of the kingdom through word and deed.[54]

Our worship tells us who we are, it tells us whose we are, and it forms us as community. We become the very body of Christ as a people who worship together. Across the globe the Anglican Church praises God in a common form binding us in community. Because of our manner of worship, the marks that make us Anglican and Episcopalian within our tradition, we find that we make a proclamation that is ancient or apostolic (reaching back to the earliest forms of Christian worship), a proclamation that is catholic or universal (stretching globally across every time zone) and present (contextually uniting people in their community with others).

Ordered for Communion

Across the Communion, as in our own Episcopal Church, we are ordered into a common life. This life is particularly and uniquely our own expression of Christianity. We have bishops who are leaders and symbols of our unity—who have a particular and unique vocation. The same can be said of priests and deacons. All of the ordered lives are in a ministry partnership with the whole body of faithful people—the baptized. In fact, those with ordered lives who work in our midst are people who are called to support the baptized in their own ministries. Together the Church (ordered and non-ordered alike) supports and—through common discernment in synods, councils, or conventions—governs the work of the Church. The ordinals of our church globally affirm this shared and mutual ministry.[55]

These common orders bridge our geographical divides. We serve together in many ministerial, missionary, and governing bodies that link us together for the purpose of our common mission of Gospel proclamation. Certainly beyond our own councils, provincial structures and General Convention, we look to the Archbishop of Canterbury, the Lambeth Conference, the Anglican Consultative Council, and the Primates Meeting as means for us to share our global communion ministry. The TEAC report says clearly that these are not places of "centralized authority," but rather places where we can see the bonds of affection and mutual ministry taking shape.[56]

Together we see our unity and our potential life as a global church and family of God. This is not to say that we do not struggle with one another. Even now we wrestle in our conversations on liturgy, women in ministry,

LGBT inclusion and marriage. And, at times, we sort out together what it means to be in ministry though we may disagree.

In our common ministries we see parallels among local organizations that network globally for both financial and spiritual support. Mission agencies are linked together more and more. In the Diocese of Texas we have more than 50 different partnerships with national and international organizations. We are strengthened when we share our life of ministry beyond our local church, and we are strengthened as relationships with diverse peoples in differing mission contexts help us renew the vision of our own ministry at home.

In the years since the colonial age of mission and the first Lambeth Conference, we have seen greater local ministry supported by the ordered life of the Church. It is easy to look over our history and see the fabric of our global life woven tightly through an ever-expanding series of new relationships. Yes, it is true that in recent years the ordered life of communion has been challenged and tested, especially with this discussion on sexuality. The West has had trouble dealing with cultures where one man has multiple wives, just as others have had difficulty with the emerging Western discourse on sexuality.

What has been truly amazing in this last decade and a half is that, despite the differences in the Episcopal Diocese of Texas, our own relationships have grown stronger. Today we are healthier than ever before. Our relationships and common work stretch not only across The Episcopal Church, but we enjoy more mission relationships with provinces and dioceses across the globe. We are a part of ministry on the ground on every continent of the globe.

We share our desire to be in communion with one another, and to support, and to share in ministry in every manner possible. I firmly believe as Anglicans and Episcopalians we are uniquely ordered as a communion—a catholic church.

A Church in Mission

The fourth way we share a common journey with Episcopalians and Anglicans is through a common mission.[57] We recognize together that our chief work is the proclamation of the Good News of Salvation through the unique witness of God in Christ Jesus. It is our Anglican and Episcopal nature to engage this work respectfully with those who are believers, seekers and even with those of other faiths or no faith. One of the unique hallmarks of our work as a church in mission is that we believe we do our mission in context. Across the Episcopal Church we do mission in different geographical, economic and cultural contexts. This mission diversity is exponential when one stops to consider the global diversity of contexts where the Anglican Communion is active.

At the center of our faith—as individuals and as a community—we share the Good News of Salvation and the unique proclamation of God in Christ Jesus with those around us. We do this in word and by example, and we understand that our lives bear witness to an incarnate God who suffered, died, and rose again. We undertake a partnership in shaping the world (not to our own devices and will) for the one who will come again.

We have certainly made a mess of this work from time to time. We have allowed national concerns and our own colonial desires to govern this mission at times. We recognize and claim our own history of abuse, self-interest and domination that has led to supporting oppression of the weak and poor.[58] This is an important part of our missionary history; nevertheless, we challenge ourselves to do better.

We make a public covenant with God that we will proclaim the Gospel in word and deed. We will see Christ in all persons. We promise to work for justice, peace, and the dignity of every human being.[59] It is important to recognize because the divisions we are working through today as a global communion are rooted in past experiences. The divisions that threaten our common work today stem from the former lack of respect for the local context in which people did their work. I believe unity will be our humble engagement in foreign partnerships that honors leaders unlike ourselves, and supports them in their mission endeavors. We will discover, I think, in this new era of global mission that we are not so much missionaries abroad but that we are pilgrims on the way to renewing our own evangelistic efforts.

So it is that we join with all of God's people, and the diverse leadership of our Anglican Communion, to do God's work of peacemaking and justice making. Today we are, as an Anglican body, seeking missionary strategies that flow out of God's reconciling love and not our own desires for power. In the past three decades our churches have been icons for reconciliation and change. Certainly, leaders come to mind who have stood against abuse of power and domination in this new missionary age.

Before us remain the challenges upon which our generation will be judged: "secularization, poverty, unbridled greed, violence, religious persecution, environmental degradation, and HIV/AIDS."[60] I believe we stand together with the potential of proclaiming a unity in Christ that is willing to help change the course of our global trajectory. I believe we are united on these issues.

Our Episcopal Witness to Unity

In our own Episcopal tradition we reflect the above common Anglican traits. We have a unique voice in the witness that the Anglican Communion presents to the world. One of the primary places you see our uniqueness modeled is in our *Book of Common Prayer* and specifically in the Baptismal Covenant. The first part of the Covenant reflects our Anglican heritage of making a faith statement prior to baptism and confirmation. This bears witness to our common and historic faith that stretches back to the first councils of the Church. While not originally meant as a document to be used in worship, the creedal statements now inhabit our lives as a weekly promise of a shared faith. This is supported in part by the first baptismal promise. It follows the creedal statements, a promise that we will continue in the apostles teaching, their fellowship, and the breaking of the bread. We bear witness to a common life molded and shaped by engagement with scripture, the ancient and apostolic witness to faith, the Church as the primary form of this fellowship, and a communal life that is Eucharist-centered.

Our Baptismal Covenant in The Episcopal Church continues with several important and unique promises. Only Anglican provinces that have adapted their services to reflect the *Book of Common Prayer* and provinces that were once part of the Episcopal Church as mission dioceses use the same formula from 1979. Today, some 16 countries make up what we call The Episcopal Church.

When we make our faith statements in worship we are saying that, as a community and as individuals, we are different from the world around us. While we may make worship changes that offer a vision into our context, we are clear that we are different from the world as well.

In almost every service the Creed is recited; it is the foundation of every Anglican service, and it is common to all rites of initiation. We make our creedal proclamation affirming the apostolic and catholic faith our church. We also do this to reaffirm our own faith. We say it to remind us that while we are people in a missionary context, we have a particular word of faith and truth to speak out in the world. We have a particular message of hope and transformation. We remind ourselves, our community, our Church, and our communion that our faith is a faith of mercy, forgiveness and unity.

We proclaim that we believe in a God who created and ordered the world for a particular purpose: beauty and relationship. We believe in a God who watches over human life and who interacts, especially within the human community. We believe in a God who desires that people be good and fair to each other and a God who says we have a responsibility to take care of those who are poor, hungry, alone or in need. We believe that Jesus Christ is the living, resurrected example of how humanity is to treat one another, and that we are to set as our goal the living of life that is most like Jesus' own. We believe it is a good thing to be happy and to feel good about one's self, but we do not believe this is the central goal in life. Moreover, as good as we are, human nature remains the same—always struggling to live as God has intended us to live. We believe that living as mere consumers can create disordered lives out of proportion with the wider needs of the world around us. We believe in a God who is a "friend" (John 15:15) and a God who is a companion along the way (Luke 24).

We believe in the kingdom of heaven, but we also believe that we are to be about bringing into reality the kingdom of God today. As Episcopalians our challenge is to hear Jesus' words of good news that the "kingdom is near." (Mark 1:9) We can see it within ourselves and our brothers and sisters. We can enact it in the world, which is our work. We remind ourselves that Jesus' work was teaching and proclaiming the Good News of the kingdom of God and curing every disease and every sickness among the people, and that he invites us with urgency, "Follow me." (Luke 4:12-23)

When we as Episcopalians step forward and choose to make our confession of faith, we choose to walk the pilgrim way with God and to live out a particular revelation found uniquely in The Episcopal Church.

The words have meaning and they have substance. As Christians who are unabashedly Episcopalian, our worship language is more than a social construct. Our words in worship combined with our faith-filled actions are sacramental and add both meaning and substance to the world around us. When we stand up and make our promises before God with the congregation and community as our witness, we create a verbal vessel of grace that makes its way through creation and draws us ever closer to the divine being and to one another.

In our faith statements, you and I are making promises about how we believe as well as statements about the kind of people we wish to become, and the kind of world in which we wish to live. When we step forward, we are proclaiming that we have a particular and unique vision of the world around us. This worldview is not formed by capitalism or some political theory. Our Episcopal world view is formed in the sacraments.

In The Episcopal Church there are two Gospel sacraments: one is the Eucharist and one is Baptism. These are considered to be Gospel sacraments because Jesus gives them to humanity and the Church as specific signs of the grace of God. We say we have seven sacraments (like the Roman Church) and we do; but Anglicans and Episcopalians recognize that the five additional sacraments were not given by Jesus Christ to the Church, but rather that the Church created them through the guiding of the Holy Spirit recognizing their power to dispense grace to the individual Christian. These sacraments are confirmation (the second half of baptism), marriage, anointing the sick, reconciliation and ordination. They are fondly referred to as the sacraments with the little "s." The Church believes they have been revealed, not by Christ but, by the living out of the kingdom of God.

Each sacrament has a special sign and is itself set aside as a vessel of God's grace. The *Book of Common Prayer* describes these other sacraments as sacraments that "evolved over time." They are not necessary but can aid in a life lived with God. We believe each of the sacraments is an outward and visible sign of inward and spiritual grace.[61]

When we step forward and make our promises as baptized Episcopalians, we say we believe in a particular kind of church. We answer the questions asked in the covenant out of our nature as Episcopalians. No other church globally (except those who began as missionary churches of the Episcopal Church) has a baptismal covenant like ours.

When we step forward to answer the Baptismal Covenant questions, we enter a community that is grounded and founded upon the ministry of Jesus Christ as a continuation of the Torah life of our Jewish faith ancestors. We claim a life lived in a particular community. So it is a continuation, if you will, of the Hebrew life revealed in what we call the Old Testament.

We are also proclaiming our faith as part of living our life. When we step forward, we are physically putting on the Church we claim as our own. We are becoming Episcopalians. We are choosing, as I think you will discover, a particular rule of life. Not unlike the communities in which the authors wrote the Gospels of Matthew, Mark, Luke and John, we make our communal life particular in our place and time as Episcopalians. We are unique and yet connected to our faith ancestors.

The baptismal promises that we proclaim begin with an affirmation of the Creed. In the Creed, the church is described as one holy, catholic and Apostolic and participates in a oneness. As a church we proclaim our unity, and we are challenged by our proclamation of unity. Some people like to talk about how the Church is not unified. Well, if we were to exist only on our own abilities and in our own manner, the Church would not be unified. The Church's unity is not dependent upon human actions. The Church is constantly enacting, in great and small measures, the unified body—the incarnational body—of Jesus Christ in the world. That is an action of God, not of human undertaking.

41

Now, humans can break it all apart and destroy it, but that does not make the Church as an expression of God's life in the world any less real. So it is that when we step forward and make our promises we make them individually and corporately. No individual ever steps forward for baptism or confirmation without the congregation promising to support them in their life in Christ as a member of The Episcopal Church, and no person ever makes their covenantal promises to God alone. So there is a unity of the Church.

The question constantly posed to the disciple making their pilgrim way is, "Am I living in that unity or not? Am I consciously seeking to be a part of that one church?"

Episcopalians believe, as did the ancient Christians, that when one is baptized one is being baptized into the body of Christ. When we present somebody to be baptized—child or adult—the vision that we see in The Episcopal Church is not of individual transformation but of the growth of the corporate body of Christ and the increase of the community itself.

Now, the questions come up. "Do you want to be baptized?" And so the person says yes or family members say yes on the child's behalf, later to be confirmed by the individual. Baptism and confirmation are a part of the same service. They are not two separate services, but when the Church began to baptize babies, the service was divided in half so that individuals could make an adult confession of faith later. Either way, there is some clarity that you desire this sacramental life or people are offering it to you, and these questions: Do you renounce Satan and all the spiritual forces of wickedness that rebel against God? Do you renounce the evil powers of this world that corrupt and destroy the creatures of God? Do you renounce all sinful desires that draw you from the love of God? Do you turn to Jesus Christ and accept him as your savior? Do you put your whole trust in his grace and love? Do you promise to follow and obey him as your lord?

You cannot get to the Baptismal Covenant without first answering these questions. We don't get to our definition of God or our promises to read scripture and participate in worship, and to strive for justice, peace and the dignity of every human being without going through these questions.

You can see that we believe in a particular God, and it is a particular world in a particular Kingdom that we are promising to be involved in. We are promising to do some very specific things. We are taking on a discipline as a Christian, and as an Episcopalian, because not everybody makes these promises in baptism.

This is part of a unique framework that is part of our Episcopal witness. When I talk about being "unabashedly" Anglican and uniquely proclaiming our Episcopal nature, this is part of it. We are united by our promises. We promise to act and speak out against spiritual forces that rebel against God and the story of God and our understanding of who God is and the world that God created. We say we will act and speak out against powers that corrupt God's creation, that move creation from sustainability to commodities for consumption, and that corrupt and destroy the creatures of God. We have clarity that we will resist desires that draw us from the love of God. We are going to aim towards Jesus Christ as the highest form of a life lived in God's community, and we are going to trust that God's love and grace will enable us to do this work.

A Hierarchy of Elements

One might ask if there is a hierarchy to the elements that make up our common life. It is my opinion that there is a hierarchy of elements and that it is important. I believe as Episcopalians and Anglicans some elements of our common life are more important than others. For instance, the Anglican Communion became an idea long before it became a reality. It was birthed out of the conflict between the breakaway colonies in our fledgling nation and a colonial empire. Today it is valued more than any other time over the last two centuries. Yet, it is still something that is becoming a reality—constantly being shaped and formed. I would add that is in large part due to our own work to help bind the global ministry of the Anglican Church together.[62]

Worship style (meaning high church or low church) has ceased to be the primary unifying principle of our communion while our common worship itself remains unifying. I have already spoken of the primary unifying elements of communion.

Theologically I rank the hierarchy of elements of conformity in this way. I would place the creeds, historic councils, the three-fold order of ministry, and prayer book worship as primary and of the utmost concern to all in the communion.

Entwined and linked to every one of these elements are the two Sacraments of the Anglican Church: Baptism and the Eucharist. They impart "grace unearned and undeserved."[63] They are the two Sacraments of the Gospel given by Christ to his Church. All other "sacramental rites evolved in the church under the guidance of the Holy Spirit."[64] The Prayer Book Catechism goes on to say that while they are a means of grace in our tradition, marriage and the other sacramental rites "are not necessary for all persons in the same way that Baptism and Eucharist are."[65]

I bring this to your attention to place marriage in its appropriate sacramental space within the life of the church locally and the communion globally. Is it important? Yes. Does the conflict on marriage merit the divergence of resources being expended through lawsuits, time, energy, the loss of membership, and the depletion of energy for the proclamation of the Gospel? No.

Unity and Interdependence

Archbishop Robert Runcie (Archbishop of Canterbury, 1080-1991), not unlike our own primates today, faced a similarly trying time for the Anglican Communion. In my view the issues that faced Archbishop Runcie locally were the disaffection between the Conservative Party of British politics and the Church of England, social change and the lack of response by governments including his own, ecumenical challenges and relationships with Rome, the ordination of women in England, and global church struggles with theological colonialism. Into this sea of change and challenge he spoke these words at the 1988 Lambeth Conference.

> ...are we being called through events and their theological interpretation to move from independence to interdependence? If we answer yes, then we cannot dodge the question of how this is to be given 'flesh': how is our interdependence articulated and made effective; how is it to be structured? ... We need to have confidence that authority is not dispersed to the point of dissolution and ineffectiveness ... Let me put it in starkly simple terms: do we really want unity within the Anglican Communion? Is our worldwide family of Christians worth bonding together? Or is our paramount concern the preservation of promotion of that particular expression of Anglicanism which has developed within the culture of our own province? ... I believe we still need the Anglican Communion. But we have reached the stage in the growth of the Communion when we must begin to make radical choices, or growth will imperceptibly turn to decay. I believe the choice between independence and interdependence, already set before us as a Communion in embryo twenty-five years ago, is quite simply the choice between unity or gradual fragmentation.[66]

What I believe Archbishop Runcie was saying is that if we are to live together in communion, as an Anglican Communion (I would even be so bold as to say an Episcopal Church), we must be willing to not only do ministry together but we must listen to one another and make our pilgrim way with one another through issues that threaten to divide us. We cannot run away from the other—for there is no communion in that at all. It is precisely when disaffected people present themselves to God in Jesus Christ that transformation occurs. Therefore, we must in some manner, some way, say "No" to the ever dividing nature of humanity that seeks to boost ego over community.

This is more eloquently stated in the Windsor Report as the authors reflect on Archbishop Runcie's statement. They write, "It is by listening to, and interacting with, voices from as many different parts of the family as possible that the church discovers what its unity and communion really mean."[67] Finding a way to be unified in mission means not walking away from one another at the exact moment in which we may actually come to know one another in an ever-deeper way. While we differ in many different ways theologically and across many different cultural contexts, it is precisely at this moment that we should embrace one another. Unity and interdependence mean that we are self-differentiated, claiming our context and view while at the same time embracing and working together with those who differ. Unity and interdependence are called "both/and" in the business world; we more commonly call it the Anglican way or the via media.

Our unity is in the creeds of the Church, the priority and formational work of scripture, apostolic worship, the threefold ordered ministry in mutual ministry with the laity, and the proclamation of the Gospel of Salvation and unique presentation of God in Christ Jesus, especially through the sacraments of Baptism and Eucharist. I will work to preserve and hand on this faith as I have received it. In all else I am willing to listen and be in relationship with the Church, though we may differ on the presenting issues of the day.

I also believe that, as the Windsor Report advises, we do, in fact, have a particular ministry for continued communion health. We, as individual churches, as a diocese within The Episcopal Church, as provinces, as primates, and as a bishop, must consider, promote and respect the common good of the Anglican Communion and its constituent churches. We must maintain our communion with fellow churches locally within The Episcopal Church and more broadly in the global Church through dialogue and in consultation with the communion leadership. This is the work of every Episcopalian and every Anglican. It is at the very core of our spiritual nature as a global Church and it is an essential ingredient of our piety.

6 ESSENTIAL FOUNDATIONS OF MARRIAGE

It is not surprising that the heirs of a denomination whose founding was forged in a context of a famous divorce would eventually find marriage and same-sex blessings complicated. When, in 1538, Henry VIII separated from what was perceived to be the Universal Church and also from Catherine of Aragon, he invented an ambivalent space in which Christians claimed to be separated from one another temporally while remaining united mystically and eschatologically through Christ. Since that time, the Anglican Church and The Episcopal Church have lived in that ambivalent space, not only doctrinally but also in their discipline. On the one hand the entirety of apostolic Christian witness insists that marriage is the lifelong union between one man and one woman.

On the other hand, the history of the relationship between secular and religious authority and their joint definition of what constitutes a marriage reveals a tolerance in Christian discipline for adapting and adjusting our Biblical, apostolic, and sacramental ideal to the circumstances of the time. Kings have not always agreed with bishops about what constitutes a marriage, but ever since at least the 12th century, bishops have won the argument. I, like the bishops before me, believe that marriage is an icon of the eternal, ideal, and real relationship between Christ and His Church. While every marriage is intended to express that icon, especially and pedagogically through the examples of Christ's ordained people, the Church has the authority to either relax or expand its understanding of how that expression is lived out through its expression of fallen humanity with certain expressions of pastoral response. As you will see in this chapter, such expansion includes divorce and remarriage of its people.[68]

I turn my attention now to the topic of traditional marriage and its most recent developments.[69] As one reads the past and current theological thoughts on marriage, there appear some common threads that are what I believe are essential foundations and common themes. Roman Catholic theologian Cardinal Walter Kasper begins his theology of marriage by asking an important question, "What is essential in marriage before we begin to speak about the connecting of families, rearing of children, and sharing of property?"[70] In many texts on marriage we find the first common thread is intimacy, which is important. It is stated in several texts that the theological significance of marriage develops from *intimate* sexual relationships of partnership, fidelity and fellowship.[71]

Yet there is more to marriage than intimacy. Kasper wrote, "The point of departure for Christian thinking about marriage today should be the aspect of mutual love and faithfulness."[72] Martin Bucer, the 16th century theologian, suggested that one of the essential goals of marriage to be "the fellowship of mutual fidelity."[73] Today our prayer book defines the goals of marriage to be mutual joy, mutual help and comfort, and for the Godly procreation and rearing of children. These are not ideals alone or without foundation in our tradition. Each statement attempts to reject the cultural ideal of romantic love as the center of marriage and redirects it, placing the emphasis on mutuality that signifies and mirrors God's love for creation. Intimacy then is always situated within a larger picture of the mission of marriage as a particular calling tied to the living out of our Baptismal Covenant with a particular individual. In other words, in The Episcopal Church we present marriage as a particular way of living out our witness of Christ and his church—it is an act of specific discipleship. Stated well by Dr. Scott Bader-Saye, "discipleship is primary and intimacy secondary."

What Bucer, Kasper and almost every theologian who has ever addressed this topic seem to reflect is the idea that marriage "has to do with God and God's will for human beings: that we are created to be partners one for another and with God in a community of mutual joy and affection for the glory of God and for the stewardship of God's creation."[74] What is essential in the sacrament of Holy Matrimony as our Episcopal Church has received it is this very notion that what we are doing is tied to the wider theme of creation and salvation history. Through the act of marriage within the Church by a heterosexual couple making a covenant with one another, tied to their baptismal promises, the whole church is able to see the revelation of the covenant relationship between God and God's people. First and foremost, the work of the couple is nothing less than living a life together that reflects God's love for His Church: this is the nuptial mystery. Our liturgy says this: "It signifies to us the mystery of the union between Christ and his Church."[75] This sentence reminds us that what we do when we are wed is to intentionally live a life that is reflective of the particular union between God and humanity.

Our theological tradition holds that the commitment of man and woman in marriage reflects God's mysterious desire for creation and humankind. When the incarnation takes place and God becomes man made manifest, heaven and earth are united. The incarnation is an "unveiling" of God's intention. The marriage of man and woman is not only a reminiscence of the first couple, but it too points towards God's intended unity of creator with creation. The "enfleshment" of the living Word proclaimed in John's Gospel (and particularly as laid out in the ancient Christian hymn that the author includes in the first chapter) is a parallel revelation to Genesis 1.[76] In the Gospels, then it is no surprise that Jesus Christ has come as the Bridegroom, the one for whom the Bride has been waiting.[77] N. T. Wright says that the nuptial mystery reflected in marriage is "the redemption of God's good world, his wonderful Creation, so that it can be the glorious thing it was made to be."[78] This is the very first common thread within the marriage tradition—it is an icon of God's love and incarnation.

There are still other threads that deserve our attention. Greg Jones captures these other essential building blocks of marriage in the text entitled *Writings on Marriage*, which was produced for the Diocese of North Carolina. These are the essential foundations of Christian marriage as I have received them, understand them, and try to articulate them to the people of the Diocese of Texas.

Theologically understood, the essence of Christian marriage is not a conversation about one's individual nature but a conversation about relationships. Christian marriage is a relationship defined by the mutual embrace of the whole person; it is an embrace of someone other than one's self. As such, the starting point for our thinking about Christian marriage is mutual love and faithfulness, and it flows out of the commandments to love God and love one another.

Christian marriage involves people who are created by God. As creatures of God, each person has dignity because he or she reflects who God made them to be, specifically the incarnation of God in Jesus Christ "through [whom] all things were made."[79] Each individual is fully human; we are not lacking anything and certainly not something that is found in marriage. Human beings do seek community though. This community of persons reflects God as Trinity. The sharing of life between two individuals bound in love reflects the perfect love that binds Father and Son. Christian marriage is a reflection of God's divine economy of love, making real in this world a reflection of who God is through mutual and shared affection.

Christian marriage involves human beings who are created from the earth. We are of earth and our bodies are flesh. Our earth-made and fleshly bodies are sexual. And as sexual creatures our sexual identity and sexual expression are very much connected both with who we are spiritually and mindfully. In Christianity, this sexual identity is fulfilled within the context of personal bonds. We understand that without these very real bonds this relationship, sexual expression and experimentation disintegrate the beauty and dignity of the human person as an individual creature of God.

Christian marriage is not a private or personal engagement. As physical beings with a bodily and sexual nature, marriage means that our relationships are public—they are communal. We make public vows as individuals and as a couple that transparently commit us not only to honor one another through love but to act in ways that dignify and provide for the other economically, socially and spiritually. Our commitment is to God first, then to one another in the context of the Christian community.

Christian marriage is a discipline and a bond that brings individual and mutual freedom. The mutual yoking of one to another in Christ offers the ability for the individual to be free to discover and become the person whom God has created. Christian marriage is not simply about loving one another, but in a deep and meaningful way it is also to love the incarnation of Christ revealed in one's spouse.

Christian marriage wherein two individuals entrust themselves to a total partnership is a form of Christian obedience. Christian marriage mirrors God's own unconditional love. In both the promises of God and the promises made in Christian marriage, the journey of life and the end of life are unknown. Faith, therefore, is essential in the success of Christian marriage. At the same time, faith in God also grows out of Christian marriage as it navigates a life of relationship, trials, tribulations, celebrations, and transformational moments. Christian marriage is therefore a sacrament in life, through which we are changed, and in which divine Grace may be experienced.

There is lastly a common thread around the significant theme of procreation in marriage. While the prayer book liturgy offers an optional prayer regarding "the gift and heritage of children," it is nevertheless an important theme.[80] From the time of Augustine forward, marriage has been seen to involve "unitive, procreative, and sacramental goods."[81] Our tradition has tended to hold that the marriage relationship as a whole needs to be open to the bearing of children, while at the same time holding that not every sexual act needs to be open to procreation. The tradition has also held that when it has not been possible to have children, then the couple has been invited to adopt or to embrace a special role of caring for the children of the church community.[82] This is a central element in our tradition because, writes Bader-Saye, "it shows the way that the love of the two, which could easily become a self-enclosed narcissism, opens up, by nature, to welcome new life—precisely through sex, the place where we are most tempted to turn our love inward rather than outward. In this way the love of the couple in marriage again mirrors the overflowing love of God that extends beyond the internal life of the Trinity to pour forth creation."[83]

So while, on the one hand, for more than 30 years The Episcopal Church and the wider Anglican Communion have been engaged in a challenging conversation about sexual ethics, especially regarding same-sex relationships in the life of the church, the essential ingredients of how we understand marriage has not changed. From before Bucer to today, we have held very basic principles of marriage that are fundamental to any conversation on the topic.

In Conversation with Charles Price and Louis Weil

The book *Liturgy for Living* written by the Rev. Dr. Charles Price and the Rev. Dr. Louis Weil, from *The Episcopal Church's Teaching Series*, offers clarity around the liturgy and nature of Christian marriage within The Episcopal Church.[84] Not only do these two contributors to the 1979 *Book of Common Prayer* offer us insight into our current liturgy of Marriage, they also offer us clarity around the theological nature of Christian marriage as our Church has practiced the sacrament.

Their article begins with these words, "Marriage is a relationship between a man and a woman for the creation and nurture of new life, and for mutual support and enjoyment."[85] We have already probed the essential theological precepts construed in this powerful and inaugural statement. Christian marriage in The Episcopal Church has and continues in my episcopate to be a relationship, a commitment between a man and a woman, for their mutual benefit and for God's benefit creating and nurturing life—for community, the support of one another, and to be for their enjoyment as well as God's. In its fidelity it reflects God's faithful covenant and the union of Christ and the Church. That is a lot to comprehend, but one can easily see that it taps into what we have already been saying. And, yet it also says a great deal more.

Price and Weil recognize that we do not arrive at this moment in our communal discourse on marriage without receiving customs and traditions from our own natural and spiritual parents. You and I come from families. Some of us are wounded from divorce; some have received and experienced healthy expressions of Christian marriage. Still others have lived within dysfunctional expressions of Christian marriage. We arrive today to read and reflect on marriage having been blessed by or having been victims of marriages that worked and did not work. We have our own cultural traditions that flow from the society in which we live and move. We are people formed within a particularly American and twenty-first-century culture. The traditions that surround marriage have so grown and diversified that a whole section of our economy is based on managing weddings.

We have seen movies from *Father of the Bride* to *Bachelor Party* where the institution and pressures surrounding marriage have influenced us through a public critique and conversation outside of the Church. So we must understand that Christian marriage, like the missionary church itself, exists within a context. This context is unique and particular and is constantly being shaped and formed by the community around us. A discussion on Christian marriage therefore includes not only the events currently shaping the world in which we live, it also must include for the Christian who is an Episcopalian the theology, liturgy and culture inherited from past church experience and the Hebrew society from which it was born.

Price and Weil capture the complexity of what we mean when we speak about marriage: "It is established by an act of intention in accordance with some custom and tradition. It constitutes families as the basic unit of society, the context for expressing the deepest of human relationships, and the normal structure within which children are born and raised. It is a completely human institution, which can be distinguished from the mating of animals ... The marriage of a man and a woman, though rooted in the natural urges of sex, is transformed by will and culture."[86]

Here marriage is transformed from simply the natural coming together of two sexes by their "will and culture." Christian marriage is hallmarked forever by the fact that one man and one woman come together and make a promise to God and one another in the midst of a community, making a covenant that is to last for all time. That community is a particular culture. It is the culture of the family of God as revealed through the Church. I believe this is an important and clarifying statement within our discussion on the topic of Christian marriage. There is the natural urge to be in community, there is an economic relationship, and there is most often property involved; and so marriage as a social construct purely does exist in culture with or without the Church.

Marriage is a contract and so local laws govern such contracts. In The Episcopal Church our theology on the matter of Christian marriage is not governed by law or by citizenship rights. Rather, it is based on our inherited scriptures, and our ancient and western traditions. It is based on our conversations over many centuries. It is the compilation of the Church's witness. So we begin with the Old Testament.

In the first stories of the Old Testament, in the very earliest of our ancient spiritual ancestral life, we see clearly that our forefathers practiced polygamy. The first instance of polygamy/bigamy in the Bible was that of Lamech in Genesis 4:19: "Lamech married two women." Several prominent men in the Old Testament were polygamists: Abraham, Jacob, David, Solomon, and others all had multiple wives. In 2 Samuel 12:8, God, speaking through the prophet Nathan, said that if David's wives and concubines were not enough, he would have given David even more. Solomon had 700 wives and 300 concubines (essentially wives of a lower status), according to 1 Kings 11:3.

Polygamy was not unusual for the Near Eastern cultures of the time in part because of the inheritance traditions of the age and the need for male heirs. Israel, in other words, was not unique. We need look no further than Jacob who took Leah and Rachel as wives and had two concubines named Billah and Zilpah (Gen. 30:1-13). Solomon was a figure who had more than a few wives.

Price and Weil wrote: "Solomon's seven hundred wives are legendary (1 Kings 11:3). One may even suspect some Oriental hyperbole!"[87] This means that the nature, complexity and makeup of what it means to be family have not always been what it is today. One man and one woman were not the norm for many centuries, and such a concept seems at odds with our current thinking around the constitution of family. Perhaps one might say that it would have been about as difficult for Solomon or Jacob to grapple with the reality of our family systems in the twenty-first century as it is for us to ponder the intricacies of family systems some 5,000+ years ago.

Polygamy was certainly the given assumption in these most ancient texts; and yet while that is foreign to our experience today in the West, the texts bring forth a special gift of theological understanding about relationships. There remain very deep and abiding scriptural truths that flow out of these early texts. The first is that creation itself "is good, human beings are good. The second is that God's covenant with God's people sets the standard for all relationships."[88] This means that relationships between husbands and wives in the Hebrew tradition and within the Israelite customs were based on these two Deuteronomic truths.

Men and women are created good and the manner in which they bring forth children is good—it is all part of God's good work. The relationship between the man and the woman, the husband and wife, is governed by the grace that governs the covenant between God and God's people. Moreover, their relationship is an example of the goodness and love of God. Price and Weil wrote: "In the second place, husbands and wives are to be related to each other with loyal love (*hesed*) of the same quality as God's loyal love to Israel."[89]

Many scholars believe that the story of creation itself, as offered in the Genesis account, places a deep understanding that our creaturely nature and our natural bonding with one another points to who God is. In the Genesis accounts, our flesh, the difference between man and woman, and their unity as partners (both in relationship one to another and sexually) reveal to the broader community who God is. Price and Weil write,

> *The story of creation in the first chapter of Genesis puts an extraordinarily high value on human sexuality. We read: "God created man in his own image, in the image of God he created him; male and female he created them" (Gen. 1:27). Sexual union is created to be one means by which human beings realize and participate in the image of God. (It is not the only one, to be sure. Marriage is not necessary to salvation.) Sexuality is therefore a matter of greatest concern for the Christian faith.*

> *On the other hand, what is designed to be a great good is often, in sin-ridden human life, a source of evil and distortion. The corruption of the best is the worst, as a familiar proverb puts it. Our sexuality is no exception. It brings soaring joy. It can also bring frustration and bitterness. In the biblical understanding of the conditions of human existence after the Fall, the relationship between man and woman comes under the curse which affects all things. What was designed as a blessing and as expression of deepest human mutuality becomes time and time again, a frustration and an opportunity for one partner to dominate the other. "...Your desire shall be for your husband, and he shall rule over you," the Genesis account reads (3:16).*

> *Under these circumstances, the understanding of marriage in Israel grew with the developing knowledge of God's ways with his people. It came to be recognized that the sexual bond between husband and wife was most secure, satisfying, and fulfilling when it was maintained in the context of a relationship marked by the kind of loyalty and faithfulness which God showed to Israel.*[90]

Price and Weil offer us an important understanding about Christian marriage in this particular part of their essay. On the one hand Christian marriage finds meaning in the goodness of God's creation. God's covenantal love is manifest in Christian marriage.

The notion of marriage inherited from our Hebrew tradition reflects the fidelity between God's people (Israel) and God. The sexual bond of marriage is part of both the goodness and the love that is part of God's creation. However, Christian marriage, as we experience it, is a sacrament well-grounded in a world after the Fall. So our experiences of domination, abuse, misuse and dysfunction do not belong to the intentions of God but rather to the sinful, broken and fallen world in which we live.

Just as the sacrament holds within it profound meaning about who God is and how God loves, we also know from experience that it is a sacrament engaged in by human beings who are often broken and hurting people. In our current time and context the reality of experience is the rule of truth. It is easy for us to believe that because we have not had a good experience with Christian marriage or because the culture doesn't choose Christian marriage that it is an institution and theology of the church that belongs in the past. I think not.

Christian marriage continues today as an icon of God's *hesed*, loyal love to his people. It is the pledge to this powerful experience of goodness and covenant love that is the strength of Christian marriage and remains so today. Christian marriage rooted in the Old Testament is about created man and created woman's goodness and faithfulness to one another (in a sexual and emotional/spiritual bond) and to God, which reflects and illustrates God's own loyalty and faithful love to all people.

The first followers of Jesus were practicing Jews, who had been formed in the teachings and instruction of the first covenant, the Old Testament. They interpreted who Jesus was based on the writings of the law and the prophets. So as they wrote the story of Jesus and managed the matters that grew out of the emerging communities of Jesus' followers, they brought to bear the ancient texts on creation and marriage. They further developed them within the context of the first century but also within the context of the revelation of Jesus Christ.

Jesus himself was clear about marriage as a lifelong faithful response to God's love and the goodness of one another. Jesus taught that marriage was difficult but that it was about monogamy and the expectation of God that it was lifelong. We look to the Gospel of Mark, chapter 10, beginning at the fifth verse, to see Jesus' teaching on marriage.

> *Jesus said, "For you hardness of heart he [Moses] wrote you this commandment. But from the beginning of creation, 'God made them male and female.' For this reason a man shall leave his father and mother and be joined to his wife, and the two shall become one flesh.' So they are no longer two but one flesh. What therefore God had joined together, let not man put asunder."*

Jesus was clear that divorce was not an option in God's eyes because divorce breaks a covenant. (Matthew 19:9).[91]

Divorce neither upholds the goodness of one another, nor does it reveal the loyal and covenantal love of a faithful God. In this teaching Jesus "establishes the permanence of the marriage bond in Christian understanding."[92] For centuries the form of Christian marriage has been between a man and a woman. It is a relationship and commitment that takes precedence over all other human relationships. It is a relationship that is higher than any previous commitments to father and mother or the family of origin.[93]

What makes the sacred bond between a man and a woman a sacrament is its faithful, unmoving commitment to one another above all else, just as God is faithful to his people. It is not the priest's blessing but rather the couple's commitment. This is significant in that it helps us understand that the church is blessing the fidelity of the couple and their commitment (even in a "fallen state") to one another.

While Price and Weil talk about the different cultural forms that arise from this understanding of family, I think it is important to consider the deeper theological challenge that Jesus presents to us in this passage. The sacrament of Christian marriage in our culture today is not threatened by the divorce rate or even the conversation around same-sex covenants (all of which we will come to in due course). The sacrament of Christian marriage is most threatened by the Church's failure to be the Church, including its failure to speak clearly and persuasively of God's loyal love to his people. As our culture becomes ever more secular, it finds little use for an accommodated church.

It is clear from Barna Group studies and the recent Pew Research Center studies that it is not God who has a problem but rather the Church.[94] Many Americans today believe that our institutions of faith are seen as ineffectual in dealing with the matters of daily life. It is a prevalent notion that the institutional church is not committed to being pastoral and relevant outside of its membership, and in moments of family crisis it is less able to help than the local therapist or counselor.[95]

The Church has not passed on or articulated well the powerful theology of God's providence and love for his people. We have not been about the work of spreading the Good News of Salvation as expressed in God's covenant relationship to his people. For me these two issues dominate the erosion of Christian marriage within our Church. We have not cared enough to teach the theology and practice of marriage as Christian discipline. We have not spoken to our people about the sacred and iconographic nature of marriage. And, so as our people experience a Church that is less concerned for their real-life struggles, they connect it with a God who seems distant, unconcerned and detached.

It is difficult to uphold a marriage of mutual love and loyalty wholly representative of God's love and faithfulness if the Church does not help the individual and couple to experience God in this manner. How can we hope to bear witness to a covenantal love when we threaten to "divorce" each other when we disagree? The Church itself has a responsibility to show God's unfailing love for creation and to be a part of people's lives in profound ways. When the Church ceases to do this most basic of pastoral ministries, we have begun to live in the hardness of our hearts and not embraced our own connection as one flesh with the community of people whom God claims as his own.

The renewal of Christian marriage does not rest upon the victory of a cultural war waged against divorce or same-sex covenants; it rests on the Church's ability to offer itself totally for the sake of those who are seeking God and God's never-failing love. How can Christian marriage withstand the trial of life in this century if the Church that institutes it does not reflect the same faithful loving care proclaimed in the Gospel?

Christian marriage is (according to the ancient scriptures and in Jesus' own words) profoundly about a man and a woman giving themselves wholly to one another. The first followers of Jesus have rooted deep within the scriptures of the Old and the New Testament theology the understanding of this self-giving as reflecting not only the creator's providence and care but Jesus' own sacrificial commitment to humanity. So it is that the liturgy of Christian marriage includes this offering of oneself completely, regardless of consequence. The relationship sought and committed to is forever and always a relationship that illustrates the love of God. The passages used in the service itself illustrate to those who witness on behalf of the whole community the meaning of the act of total self-giving and how it is tied to the New Testament's proclamation of Christ's love for the world and the Church.

In the 1 Corinthians passage we see that love is an essential ingredient to the marital relationship. This is not a romantic notion of love. On the contrary, Paul is speaking of one of the gifts of God's Holy Spirit. The gift that binds community together is love and it does not originate within the relationship or community but comes from without and from God alone as gift. So too for marriage it echoes the broader unifying spirit of the Christian community that is always and forever held together not by its own force of will but rather by the Holy Spirit's gift of Love. Chapter 13 is a beautiful passage that is rooted in the context of teaching about community. It is a powerful witness by Paul. It speaks as much to the unity of the Christian Church with its diverse opinions as it does for the marital couple who are assuming a vow of unity in the worst of times, in poverty, and in sickness. They, like our diocesan community, are/will be held together by God's faithful love alone. Paul writes in 1 Corinthians 13:1-13:

If I speak in the tongues of mortals and of angels, but do not have love, I am a noisy gong or a clanging cymbal. And if I have prophetic powers, and understand all mysteries and all knowledge, and if I have all faith, so as to remove mountains, but do not have love, I am nothing. If I give away all my possessions, and if I hand over my body so that I may boast, but do not have love, I gain nothing.

Love is patient; love is kind; love is not envious or boastful or arrogant or rude. It does not insist on its own way; it is not irritable or resentful; it does not rejoice in wrongdoing, but rejoices in the truth. It bears all things, believes all things, hopes all things, endures all things.

Love never ends. But as for prophecies, they will come to an end; as for tongues, they will cease; as for knowledge, it will come to an end. For we know only in part, and we prophesy only in part; but when the complete comes, the partial will come to an end.

When I was a child, I spoke like a child, I thought like a child, I reasoned like a child; when I became an adult, I put an end to childish ways. For now we see in a mirror, dimly, but then we will see face to face. Now I know only in part; then I will know fully, even as I have been fully known. And now faith, hope, and love abide, these three; and the greatest of these is love.

The passage from Paul's letter to the Ephesians, which may also be chosen, has similar themes. In it Paul is describing his own experience of God's faithfulness and his desire to share it with the Ephesians. He is praying that those in Ephesus may be granted the very same spirit of God's love. He prays that they as community may be bound together in God's faithful love that the world will know Christ and his mission to gather all people to himself.

Again the gift of love and power to be bound one to another does not generate within the couple but is a gift; and it is not for the sake of the couple, but for the sake of the Gospel mission. Not unlike couples we marry, our church community receives the same blessing of love from a faithful God that we might be one for the sake of our witness to the world around us. Paul writes in Ephesians 3:14-21:

For this reason I bow my knees before the Father, from whom every family in heaven and on earth takes its name. I pray that, according to the riches of his glory, he may grant that you may be strengthened in your inner being with power through his Spirit, and that Christ may dwell in your hearts through faith, as you are being rooted and grounded in love, pray that you may have the power to comprehend, with all the saints, what is the breadth and length and height and depth, and to know the love of Christ that surpasses knowledge, so that you may be filled with all the fullness of God. Now to him who by the power at work within us is able to accomplish abundantly far more than all we can ask or imagine, to him be glory in the church and in Christ Jesus to all generations, forever and ever. Amen.

In the second passage for Ephesians that may be chosen, Paul invites the community of Ephesus to be at work forgiving one another for when they do this as beloved people of God they reveal the God who forgives. It recognizes the sinfulness that is in us and offers a vision of a virtuous life lived for God. Paul writes in Ephesians 5:1-7, 5:15-20:

Therefore be imitators of God, as beloved children, and live in love, as Christ loved us and gave himself up for us, a fragrant offering and sacrifice to God. Be careful then how you live, not as unwise people but as wise, making the most of the time, because the days are evil. So do not be foolish, but understand what the will of the Lord is. Do not get drunk with wine, for that is debauchery; but be filled with the Spirit, as you sing psalms and hymns and spiritual songs among yourselves, singing and making melody to the Lord in your hearts, giving thanks to God the Father at all times and for everything in the name of our Lord Jesus Christ.

In the passage from Colossians, which is an option for the marriage ceremony, Paul is speaking to the community and inviting them to remember who has chosen them—God. It is God that has brought them together and claimed them. God has raised them to a new life of faith and they are to seek a heavenly reflection in life. They are to seek to be God's chosen and beloved. Therefore, they are to clothe themselves with Christ's nature in their relationships. The church, like the married couple hearing this lesson, is to allow Christ's nature to rule our relationships and actions. Paul writes in Colossians 3:12-21:

As God's chosen ones, holy and beloved, clothe yourselves with compassion, kindness, humility, meekness, and patience. Bear with one another and, if anyone has a complaint against another, forgive each other; just as the Lord has forgiven you, so you also must forgive. Above all, clothe yourselves with love, which binds everything together in perfect harmony. And let the peace of Christ rule in your hearts, to which indeed you were called in the one body. And be thankful. Let the word of Christ dwell in you richly; teach and admonish one another in all wisdom;

and with gratitude in your hearts sing psalms, hymns, and spiritual songs to God. And whatever you do, in word or deed, do everything in the name of the Lord Jesus, giving thanks to God the Father through him.

In the First letter from John to his community, he invites them to reject the spirit that is not the spirit of love. The spirit of love is the spirit of the followers of Jesus. The loving person is a person from God and reveals God's nature. Again in this passage we catch glimpses of the Gospel of John and the nuptial mystery whereby we are to love as God loved and gave himself for us. The couple is inspired to mirror a loving Christian community, which is itself a reflection of God's desire for unity with humankind. In 1 John 4:7ff, we find these words:

Beloved, let us love one another, because love is from God; everyone who loves is born of God and knows God. Whoever does not love does not know God, for God is love. God's love was revealed among us in this way: God sent his only Son into the world so that we might live through him. In this is love, not that we loved God but that he loved us and sent his Son to be the atoning sacrifice for our sins. Beloved, since God loved us so much, we also ought to love one another. No one has ever seen God; if we love one another, God lives in us, and his love is perfected in us. By this we know that we abide in him and he in us, because he has given us of his Spirit.

And we have seen and do testify that the Father has sent his Son as the Savior of the world. God abides in those who confess that Jesus is the Son of God, and they abide in God. So we have known and believe the love that God has for us. God is love, and those who abide in love abide in God, and God abides in them.

The passage, from Ephesians 5:21-33, gives a sense of the profound image of Christ's love that is expected in both the sacramental covenant of marriage and in the relationship of man and woman one to another.

Be subject to one another out of reverence for Christ. Wives, be subject to your husbands as you are to the Lord. For the husband is the head of the wife just as Christ is the head of the church, the body of which he is the Savior. ... Husbands, love your wives, just as Christ loved the church and gave himself up for her, in order to make her holy by cleansing her with the washing of water by the word, so as to present the church to himself in splendor, without a spot or wrinkle or anything of the kind—yes, so that she may be holy and without blemish. In the same way, husbands should love their wives as they do their own bodies. He who loves his wife loves himself.

Like Price and Weil and a host of Episcopalians, theologians and laity alike, we "regret the lack of mutuality between man and woman expressed in this passage."[96]

"Many of us today would say that husbands and wives should be subject to each other and should give themselves to each other, as Christ loved the church and gave himself up for it. We believe that this mutuality is an implication of Christian love, which has gradually become clear as Christian people have lived into the meaning of the Christian mystery."[97]

We understand, therefore, that the image for Christian marriage, beyond the witness of the Old Testament, is the exemplifying character of Christ's complete self-giving.

There can be no question that the model for Christian community, of which marriage is a microcosm, is the complete bountiful and generous nature of God in Christ Jesus and his "agape" love.[98] As people ponder the implications of God and Christ's generous love for them within the Christian community, they are given an image of God whose love is complete for his Church. They also see God's fidelity to his creation, his desire to be united with humankind, and his invitation to live in this sacred and holy community that is bound together through the Holy Spirit's gift of love.[99] For Christians who choose to marry, meaning is found in fidelity to another, fidelity that is an icon of God's "unswerving faithfulness, revealed by Christ, which God has for his people."[100]

What I find interesting is that Price and Weil wrote in 1979 that when a Christian community's conviction of God's faithfulness wavers, the nature of the wedding vow and the security of its promises will, too. They write:

The love of God in Christ, agape, which is faithful to death, redeems sexual love, eros, and makes it capable of bearing the meaning it was designed in creation to have; capable of making the union of male and female to be the image of God. This capacity of Christian marriage to be a communicating symbol of god's own life is so potent that marriage is commonly called a sacramental act.[101]

Christian marriage has, as we have received the teaching of the Church, forever been and will continue to be an icon of God's love for the world.

Christian marriage itself, the sacramental act of blessing individuals in a rite, is not an invention of Jesus. There is not a rite of marriage—Israelite or Christian—recorded in the Bible. The wedding of Cana—the story of Jesus' first miracle—in John's Gospel simply speaks of the context of the miracle but records no rite of marriage. This means that we are left without biblical texts in which to guide the construction of the ritual of Christian marriage.

And we are given little if no real help in understanding the first rites of Christian blessings of marriages if they occurred prior to the third century. There may have been some movement of marriage in the ritual world of early Christianity, but it is clear that there was none in the Christian texts and traditions that survive today.

Price and Weil point out that "Ignatius required a couple seeking marriage to get the bishop's permission, and Tertullian in the third century indicated that a couple's marriage would be blessed at a celebration of the Eucharist. In each case the implication is that the actual marriage ceremony took place in accordance with existing local customs."[102] We also know that the ancient tradition of blessing the civil ceremony, when practiced, was done during the Eucharist, a tradition that continues today.

It has been the custom in Europe, and in many places is more common today, that the Church blesses only what the civil servants have already pronounced legally. It was for a long time the work of the local government to deal with the binding of men and women in contracts of marriage. The church simply blessed two people wishing to make a public commitment because of their own faithful response to God's providence and faithful love.

We also know that it was not until the Middle Ages that we had a description of a marriage liturgy. This is not to say that faithful men and women were not living in relationships or even that they didn't consider their family's life to be an extension of God's love or even the reflection of the Church. We do know though that there was not an expectation that marriage took place in the Church.

As we review the development of Christian marriage, it is clear that it grew out of the Church taking on the civil ceremony, not the other way around. What we are describing is the fact that Christian men and women have always come to the Church seeking its blessing for life, children, crops, the safe return of men at war, and for healing an ailing relative. It was a natural progression as the Church took a greater role in governing and Christians got married that the two events, civil and religious, were comingled.

Price and Weil wrote: "When the church at last did take over the marriage ceremony, it really functioned as the civil authority, church and state being coterminous at this period of history [ninth century]. The priest was understood to function as a *witness* of the couple's vows as well as the church's representative to bless the couple. The marriage rite itself embodied local customs. Some of the features of the Prayer Book service most familiar to Episcopalians originate in northern England. The father's giving away of the bride, for example, belongs in this category. The giving of a ring as a symbol of the vow is a widespread European custom, but it is by no means universal."[103]

In our country the ordained are permitted to function as a civil officer witnessing the exchange of vows according to the license of the state. In many European countries, if you wish to get married, you are married in a civil ceremony and only after is there a blessing of the civil union. According to Title 1.18.1 of the Constitution and Canons of The Episcopal Church, every member of the clergy is required to "conform to the laws of the State governing the creation of the civil status of marriage, and also to the laws of the Church governing the solemnization of Holy Matrimony."

The 1979 *Book of Common Prayer*, not surprisingly, reflects the culmination of our theology regarding marriage, the liturgical history of the rite dating to the ninth century, and the civil contract of its day. It is a ceremony bathed in sacramental theology that is essentially the exchange of vows and a blessing all within the pro anaphora (or beginning) of the Eucharist. Like baptism and regular Sunday worship, the vows and the blessing take place within the liturgy of the word.

The beginning of the service is clear and the opening words by the celebrant affirm everything that I have already laid out. The vows and the blessing are certainly present but so are the words about union, bond and covenant, God's reflection, creation, the mystery of sacrament, the whole commitment of self for the other, mutual benefit, reflecting the family of the church and God's family and the sharing of the love of God.

> *The bond and covenant of marriage was established by God in creation, and our Lord Jesus Christ adorned this manner of life by his presence and first miracle at a wedding in Cana of Galilee. It signifies to us the mystery of the union between Christ and his Church…*

> *The union of husband and wife in heart, body, and mind is intended by God for their mutual joy; for the help and comfort given one another in prosperity and adversity; and, when it is God's will, for the procreation of children and their nurture in the knowledge and love of the Lord.*[104]

It is my opinion that we do not undo the meaning of marriage between two heterosexual individuals as we have received it over these many years by proposing the blessing of same-sex relationships. For those who are married, this liturgy brings meaning and covenant to their common life and their life with God. We cannot and we do not undo something that is of great importance in the lives of many people, which is theologically of value, just because we are seeking to reach out to do something new for others. Marriage as a rite and sacrament of the Church continues today as a sign of God's covenant to his people. It should continue so even as our Church expands its inclusion of LGBT peoples. This is really what the Church is doing. The Church is not doing away with something so much as it is expanding it for the benefit of those who wish to model unity and fidelity in their lives.

Marriage between one man and one woman has meaning for me as a bishop, theologian and husband. These are the promises that my wife and I made to one another and to God. Our promises and the promises of hundreds of thousands more cannot be undone by the vision of something new. It is for this reason that I will continue to hold what is now considered the traditional understanding of marriage as central to the life and ministry of the Church. And yet, we are invited to understand the importance of marriage for others. Marriage is not meant solely for my wife and myself— others are called into this vocation of unity.

Remarriage - Making Room for the Pastoral in the Midst of Reality

Remarriage itself recognizes by its very nature the painful loss of a spouse through death or by virtue of a life together that no longer reflects our understanding of traditional marriage's sacramental iconography as a vehicle for God's love and grace. Divorce is a "defeat" of the Christian vision of marriage. However, remarriage offers hope for a renewed commitment and covenant between two people who have let go of a previous life commitment.

Sometime after Charles Price and Louis Weil's essay was published, Weil took a moment and offered a reflection on the changing nature of marriage over time and the shifts he had witnessed in his own lifetime.

> *Two thousand years of Christian experience have taught us that despite the best of intentions, some marriages are not healthy. Some way has to be provided to dissolve them in these cases the breakup of a marriage may be the least of evils, but it is a defeat for the Christian vision of what marriage can be to a couple who undertake it. Christian marriage must intend it to be permanent when they exchange their vows.*[105]

This paper is primarily concerned with the discourse and current divide over the blessing of same-sex relationships and our search for a common vision of unity for the sake of mission. I do not think that we can fully ponder these things if we do not take a moment here to say that this is not the first time that the "sacrament of marriage" has been tested by prevailing cultural norms.

Our Church also faced similar questions and challenges as growing numbers of people were divorced in this country. The first time that the General Convention addressed this matter was at the 1808 meeting.[106] That joint resolution provided:

> *Resolved, That it is the sense of this Church, that it is inconsistent with the law of God, and the Ministers of this Church, therefore, shall not unite in matrimony any person who is divorced, unless it be on account of the other party being guilty of adultery.*[107]

Sixty years later the Convention of 1868 passed further canonical legislation regarding divorce and remarriage. That canon provided:

> *No minister of this Church shall solemnize Matrimony in any case where there is a divorced wife or husband of either party still living; but this Canon shall not be held to apply to the innocent party in a divorce for the cause of adultery, or to parties once divorced but seeking to be united again.*[108]

This was repealed by the Convention of 1877 and exchanged. The new canon was stricter not only binding the priests but also the people involved. The 1877 text was virtually the same except it gave provision for annulment.[109]

The Convention of 1904 allowed the innocent party to a divorce (caused by adultery) to be remarried within the Church. This, however, while accepted here in The Episcopal Church, did not follow other canon law in the communion and was out of sync with the canon law of the Church of England. It also added in this version a one-year waiting period. And the parties were to bring satisfactory evidence regarding the facts to the ecclesiastical authorities for a ruling. This ensured that the individuals and clergy were operating within the canon of the church.[110] It also permitted remarriage in those instances of annulment, "i.e., the cause of the divorce arose prior to the marriage, by a civil court."[111] In 1922, more definitions were added to ensure equity between clergy and laity regarding remarriage.

Almost 10 years later, at the Convention of 1931, while keeping the basic form and intent of the 1904 canon with its successive modifications, the Convention added a provision for grounds upon which a former marriage annulled or dissolved by a civil court could be declared null and void by a bishop. The impediments to marriage were stated clearly as:

Consanguinity
Lack of free consent
Mistake as to the identity of either party
Mental deficiency sufficient to prevent intelligent choice
Insanity of either party
Failure of either party to have reached the age of puberty
Undisclosed impotence
Venereal disease in either party and
Facts which would make the marriage bigamous[112]

The canon also said:

> *Any person whose former marriage has been annulled or dissolved by a civil court and pronounced null by the Bishop, may be married by a Minister of this Church as if he had never previously been married.*

The Conventions of 1937–1943 continued to refine the language and form of the canon. In 1946 more impediments were added:

> *The Convention of 1946 expanded the list of Impediments, which now constituted a bar to first marriage, as well as a basis for permission to remarry. The additional Impediments were: "Concurrent contract inconsistent with the contract constituting canonical marriage," and "Attendant conditions: error as to the identity of either party, fraud, coercion or duress, or such defects of personality as to make competent or free consent impossible." The Matthean exception was not mentioned. This Convention also amended the canon pertaining to remarriage by imposing a one-year waiting period after any civil court annulment or dissolution. In the case of a prior marriage, the bishop was tasked to determine whether the parties to the proposed remarriage "intend a true Christian marriage," and whether any of the canonical Impediments are shown to exist or to have existed which manifestly establish that no marriage bond as the same is recognized by this Church exists ...[113]*

In 1973 the Convention removed the canonical prohibition against the remarriage of members of the Church whose former spouse was still living, and whose prior marriage was valid from its inception. The provision that most of us take for granted today was a long, painful development. It took over 177 years for the Church to make up its mind about the nature of remarriage and how it would deal with an emerging growth in divorces among its members. These were not only discussion and division on canon law.

We as a Church came to an understanding that when individuals in a marriage no longer embrace the whole other person through a mutual love, or recognize their partners as God's creation, or treat one another with dignity, or as fully human, or through the appreciation of each other's beauty, or by living out symbolically the nature of the Trinity, such marriages are dissolved.

Moreover, while the Church recognizes marriage as one woman and one man joined together in perpetuity, when that marriage ends in divorce, it is a possibility that either or both parties may, in fact, seek out this life-giving relationship with another human being. The Church changed its understanding about relationships in order to make pastoral room for those who found new bonds of love that led to a desire to be married.

We cannot underestimate the ferocity of the battles that ensued. There are people today who are very injured from that era. Still others who are members in other churches with a different understanding than our own often find hope in our Church because of the pastoral room we have made in our tradition for such situations.

Today marriage and remarriage is a regular part of our life as a church. The Episcopal Church in the Diocese of Texas did more than 101 remarriages in 2014 alone. That is a lot in my opinion. In point of fact, a number of those were third marriages.

Moreover, because it is a part of our common life today, we may forget that in the scriptures Jesus speaks particularly against this, as do the Epistles. In fact, there is more New Testament scripture against remarriage than there is on other sexual exploits. I say this because we all have our own canon of scripture. Typically, in our ever-human way, seek to make our argument out of the scripture we know.

We should be aware that the Church has changed its mind on divorce and remarriage considerably since the time of Jesus. Yet, I would offer we did so out of our pastoral concern and desire to offer redeeming grace to those who sought relief from marriages they believed failed and an ever-new opportunity for transformation through the gift of marriage.

We as a church have come to believe that remarriage (though clearly against scripture) mirrors God's own unconditional love. So it is that we might wonder how is it that we can make room for a pastoral response to fallenness and not at the same time make a positive pastoral response by expanding these rites for the sake of fidelity?

7 WE ARE NOT OF ONE MIND

As many of you know, I was brought up in an Episcopal household. I went to church weekly. I went to Sunday school as a child and as an adult. I read and reread scripture as I grew older. I participated fully in the life of the Episcopal Church. I bring this up because of the awakening that I had when I went to seminary.

I believed that somehow there had been one monolithic church, undivided, until the Reformation, when the Church of England was born along with other reformed churches. I believed that we in the Anglican and specifically the Episcopal Church reflected a unified faith that was only one step from Rome and its unified faith that stretched back to Jesus. I awakened to the reality that Christians have been fighting with one another for ages and over things that I just assumed we had always believed.

It did not take long after Jesus' death for the Church to begin to debate the different books of the Bible—which should be in and which should be left out. Then we fought over God's oneness, or his Trinitarian nature. Then we fought over the Holy Spirit. We fought over the nature of the incarnation. We argued about the nature of the Church and its authority, who were the saints. We argued over the nature of salvation. We did all of that long before the Middle Ages, sometimes hashing and rehashing the arguments. We argued and continue to argue over baptism and the Eucharist. We have argued over the end times, and we have argued about the meaning of the kingdom of God. We have argued about the orders of ministry, the pope, power and the number of sacraments. We have argued over how many angels may fit on the end of a pin, and whether we should have candles on the altar. We have waged bloody civil wars over these beliefs and many a Christian has killed another for the sake of their conscience.

My view before seminary was naive on my part. I will tell you that as a priest and now as a bishop I find such naiveté prevalent throughout our Church. People believe as I did and so they were sure that the local church custom, their experience, and local story are universal. And, because this notion is prevalent, we have a false sense of our past and our present. We have a nostalgic sense that somehow we have never really fought over things before, or that somehow we were unified until just recently. When we have this view, we are more often than not disappointed and we are frustrated as the slow moving church navigates conflict in our modern world. This is heightened by the pace of our culture, the global nature of communication, and the rampant miscommunication of any one person's view as the all-encompassing truth.

The reality is that today, just as in the past, we face a particular turning point. How do we live together and do our ministry within a Church that is divided on the nature of sexuality and marriage?

Adiaphora

I think it is appropriate here to consider a wider communion view of the situation regarding differing viewpoints. The wider communion has sought to manage its diverse nature in recent times by using a term called *adiaphora*. Strictly speaking, *adiaphora* means "things that do not make a difference, matters regarded as nonessential, issues about which one can disagree without dividing the Church." Here is the first place in which our divided church meets.

The classic biblical statements of this principle can be found in Paul's letter to the Romans (14:1-15:13) and again when he writes his first letter to the Corinthians in chapters 8-10. Both these extensive passages reveal Paul's wrestling with inherited traditions that are threatening to divide the communities. Paul offers a vision of a community that is bound in the God who is love and embraces us. Each argument might be characterized by the very first line in his letter to the Romans in chapter 14.

Paul writes: "Welcome those are weak in the faith, but not for the purpose of quarrelling over opinions." Later he continues that our life and the life of our community are lived for God and God alone (Romans 14:7). He is struggling, even in the earliest years of Christianity, with the nature of what is essentially important and what is not. The Windsor Report describes this notion of what is essential carefully as it seeks to navigate the current division in the Church. Here I want to give some space to this and quote directly from the Windsor Report as I believe it is essential for understanding the position I will later lay before you as our strategy.

There, [Romans 14 and I Corinthians 8ff] in different though related contexts, Paul insists that such matters as food and drink (eating meat and drinking wine, or abstaining from doing so; eating meat that had been offered to idols, or refusing to do so), are matters of private conviction over which Christians who take different positions ought not to judge one another. They must strive for that united worship and witness which celebrate and display the fact that they are worshipping the same God and are servants of the same Lord.

This principle of "adiaphora" was invoked and developed by the early English Reformers, particularly in their claim that, in matters of Eucharistic theology, specific interpretations (transubstantiation was particularly in mind) were not to be insisted upon as "necessary to be believed," and that a wider range of interpretations was to be allowed. Ever since then, the notion of "adiaphora" has been a major feature of Anglican theology, over against those schools of thought, both Roman and Protestant, in which even the smallest details of belief and practice are sometimes regarded as essential parts of an indivisible whole.

This does not mean, however, that either for Paul or in Anglican theology all things over which Christians in fact disagree are automatically to be placed into the category of "adiaphora." It has never been enough to say that we must celebrate or at least respect "difference" without further ado. Not all "differences" can be tolerated. (We know this well enough in the cases of, say, racism or child abuse; we would not say "some of us are racists, some of us are not, so let's celebrate our diversity"). This question is frequently begged in current discussions, as for instance when people suggest without further argument, in relation to a particular controversial issue, that it should not be allowed to impair the Church's unity, in other words that the matter in question is not as serious as some suppose. In the letters already quoted, Paul is quite clear that there are several matters – obvious examples being incest (1 Corinthians 5) and lawsuits between Christians before non-Christian courts (1 Corinthians 6) – in which there is no question of saying "some Christians think this, other Christians think that, and you must learn to live with the difference." On the contrary: Paul insists that some types of behavior are incompatible with inheriting God's coming kingdom, and must not therefore be tolerated within the Church. "Difference" has become a concept within current postmodern discourse which can easily mislead the contemporary western church into forgetting the principles, enshrined in scripture and often rearticulated within Anglicanism, for distinguishing one type of difference from another.

The question then naturally arises as to how one can tell, and indeed as to who can decide, which types of behavior count as "adiaphora" and which do not. For Paul, the categories are not arbitrary, but clearly distinct. For instance: that which would otherwise separate Jew and Gentile within the Church is "adiaphora." That which embodies and expresses renewed humanity in Christ is always mandatory for Christians; that which embodies the dehumanizing turning-away-from-God which Paul characterizes with such terms as "sin," "flesh," and so on, is always forbidden. This, of course, leaves several questions unanswered, but at least sketches a map on which further discussions may be located.

To this end, we note that, though Paul's notion of "adiaphora" does indeed envisage situations where particular aspects of lifestyle are associated with particular cultures, he never supposes that human culture in the abstract is simply "neutral," so that all habits of thought and life within a particular culture are to be regarded either as "inessential" or for that matter "to be supported and enhanced." When we put the notion of "adiaphora" together with that of inculturation (see above in paragraphs 32, 67, 85), this is what we find: in Paul's world, many cultures prided themselves on such things as anger and violence on the one hand and sexual profligacy on the other. Paul insists that both of these are ruled out for those in Christ. Others prided themselves on such things as justice and peace; Paul demonstrated that the gospel of Jesus enhanced and fulfilled such aspirations. The Church in each culture, and each generation, must hammer out the equivalent complex and demanding judgments.

Even when the notion of "adiaphora" applies, it does not mean that Christians are left free to pursue their own personal choices without restriction. Paul insists that those who take what he calls the "strong" position, claiming the right to eat and drink what others regard as off limits, must take care of the "weak," those who still have scruples of conscience about the matters in question — since those who are lured into acting against conscience are thereby drawn into sin. Paul does not envisage this as a static situation. He clearly hopes that his own teaching, and mutual acceptance within the Christian family, will bring people to one mind. But he knows from pastoral experience that people do not change their minds overnight on matters deep within their culture and experience.

Whenever, therefore, a claim is made that a particular theological or ethical stance is something "indifferent," and that people should be free to follow it without the Church being thereby split, there are two questions to be asked. First, is this in fact the kind of matter which can count as "inessential," or does it touch on something vital? Second, if it is indeed "adiaphora," is it something that, nevertheless, a sufficient number of other Christians will find scandalous and offensive, either in the sense that they will be led into acting against their own consciences or that they will be forced, for conscience's sake, to break fellowship with those who go ahead? If the answer to the latter question is "yes," the biblical guidelines insist that those who have no scruples about the proposed action should nevertheless refrain from going ahead. Thus the notion of "adiaphora" is brought back into its close relationship with that of "subsidiarity," the principle that matters in the Church should be decided as close to the local level as possible. A distinction is drawn between trivial issues about which nobody would dream of consulting the great councils of the Communion, and more serious matters which no local church has the right to tamper with on its own. The two notions of "adiaphora" and "subsidiarity" work together like this: the clearer it is that something is "indifferent" in terms of the Church's central doctrine and ethics, the closer to the local level it can be decided; whereas the clearer it is that something is central, the wider must be the circle of consultation. Once again, this poses the question: how does one know, and who decides, where on this sliding scale a particular issue belongs? In many cases an obvious prima facie case exists of sufficient controversy, both locally and across the Communion, to justify, if only for the reasons in the previous paragraph, reference to the wider diocese or province, or even to the whole Communion.

Not least because of the recurring questions about "who decides" in these matters, the twin notions of "adiaphora" and "subsidiarity" need to be triangulated with the questions of authority, and particularly the authority of scripture on the one hand and of decision-makers in the Church on the other. This brings us back from consideration of the nature of diversity within communion to the bonds of unity which hold that communion together, and so to complete the circle of this account of what our communion actually is and how it functions and flourishes as it seeks to serve the mission of God in the world.[114]

I think what the report and Paul make clear is that even in our differences we are to be primarily committed to the community, so the questions about eating or drinking are NOT private matters. Neither are they the most important and unifying element of the community. In the end there are some things that are more important than others in the sustaining of the community in mission. I believe Paul wanted his communities to understand that our personal convictions on certain matters need to take a backseat to the common good and the mission of the gospel.

I make the case that both the traditional and the progressive side of the conflict on sexuality would argue that marriage is **not *adiaphora*** but rather one of the essential ingredients to community life.

They would, however, disagree on who gets to decide such matters. The traditional side would lean toward the scripture and documents like the Windsor Report as the guiding authority and press for waiting until there is broad communion support for blessings; this they have done. From the progressive perspective the choice is located not within the Instruments of Communion but within the province itself (referring to The Episcopal Church, for instance), which is why they have pressed forward towards full inclusion regarding the rite of marriage.

Within our Church there are a growing number of individuals who would indeed say that our uniformity on the sacrament of marriage is indeed *adiaphora*. There are a number of leaders who do not see our common and uniform theology on this (non-Gospel) sacrament as essential for the unity and mission of the Church. These leaders see this issue as similar to the dietary issues raised in Paul's epistles, or as described in Acts. There is a higher good at stake they would argue. Meanwhile, still others (progressives and traditionalists) believe this is an essential teaching of the church.

The church is not of one mind about whether we must all agree in order to remain unified.

We are fallen creatures and one of the things that we do is delegitimize the other. We certainly have been doing this quite well as we have approached the issues of sexuality. People on both sides of the sexuality issue have sought to alienate the other and say, "You are not in." "You are not just." "You should leave." "You are not a true believer." "You are caving to the culture." And so the two sides have drawn their lines in the sand and demarcated TRUE community.

What we deny in acting this way is that God has brought us (despite our differences) together for the sake of his Gospel and for the mission of the Church. We cannot unmake ourselves. "Those whom God has joined together let no one put asunder."[115] Over the centuries what we have learned is that the Church is one and apostolic not by its uniformity of belief but by the bond of love between Christ and Christians as they live out the apostolic witness to Jesus Christ. Augustine of Hippo said that it remains *one* by continuing to receive grace from God. It is catholic because universally it is the "root of charity in the bond of peace and in the fellowship of unity."[116]

I am not arguing that Augustine would be in favor of blessing same-sex relationships; in fact, I think he would have a difficult time understanding our view of anthropology and sexuality. I am saying that the basics of Augustine's argument remind us that our unity is not based upon what a person does or even believes. His argument reminds us that our unity as church is constantly dependent upon grace and upon Jesus Christ. It reminds us that the argument before us really may be *adiaphora* or nonessential when it comes to the unifying principles of mission by the Church. In a way we are repeating our Donatist heresy by believing if we don't all agree on sexuality we are somehow not the "true" church.[117]

Nevertheless, our thinking today about purity of belief is predominant, especially in the midst of our division. Our younger leadership, in the tradition of Augustine, does not see the discourse on sexuality as necessary for the saving of their own souls, the transformation of their own lives, or the unity of their community for the sake of common mission as Anglicans. While some would disagree, my guess is that there are, in fact, many more of every age who agree.

That being said, it is here in the emerging discourse over our polity and the context of *adiaphora* that we have a conflict between two very distinct sides on sexuality, both of which exist within our Church. It is my perspective that both ends of the theological spectrum believe that a common and uniform theology on marriage is *necessary* and *required* for unity. It is an issue that is present within the wider conflict on sexuality, marriage and ordination of gay and lesbian people.

The issue of *adiaphora*, while clearly articulated in the Windsor Report, is one that has existed for a long time on many other and diverse issues, and dates back to the earliest beginnings of the global communion. Culture, mission strategy, theology, and liturgy have all woven themselves into this complex conversation on what is necessary for communion and what is not necessary. A shared unanimity by all individual members of the Church is neither possible nor necessary for unity in mission.

The Traditional View on Marriage

The Lambeth Conferences of 1988, 1998, and 2008 have urged churches of the Anglican Communion to engage in an intentional process of listening to the experiences of gay and lesbian persons and exploring our pastoral ministry to them. There have been sharp disagreements between the opposing sides of this conflict.

Our life within the Communion has been strained because of the fight, and we have been repeatedly encouraged to listen to one another and to the "other's" viewpoint. It is important to listen to the view of our neighbor if we are to understand where we are as a church and to understand where others stand. This can be difficult work but it is important work. I find reflecting on another's opinion is important in understanding my location on the map, and it helps me to understand the place I currently inhabit.

The House of Bishops Theology Committee invited both sides of the divide on sexuality to make a case for their view with the expectation that we as individual bishops would have a greater sense and understanding about where we stood in the midst of community.[118] I think it was a helpful exercise and one worth thinking about here. To that end what follows is a synopsis of the traditional view on marriage as given in the paper.

The traditionalist argument for marriage begins by stating concern about the future of the faith. Traditionalists write in their paper, "Conservatives also share the skepticism voiced by non-Western church leaders about the agenda of modern liberals, because so often the attitudes toward a revision of traditional views of sex and marriage are linked with liberal views of biblical authority, theological heterodoxy, and a general tendency to water down the basis and nature of Christian attitudes and way of life. This would generate a Christianity that, by not being countercultural enough, becomes unfaithful to the Gospel."

The traditionalist is in favor of the current practice of marriage and remarriage. They argue that if there is genuine error in their thinking then by all means the Church should reform itself and make room for the blessing of same-sex relationships. And, so their paper argues out that, in fact, from their perspective, the church is not in error.

Furthermore, they make the case that there is no requirement to abolish practices and institutions that develop in accordance with reason and tradition when they are not in contradiction with Holy Scripture. They base this upon Richard Hooker's text *Ecclesiastical Polity.* They also rest upon Hooker's natural law.

This then leads to their argument that the scripture is uniquely authoritative for basic Christian belief and practice and that it offers clarity on the nature of marriage as union between one man and one woman, which is at the heart of the traditional perspective. They say that the traditional and liberal students of scripture simply read the texts differently.

They note also that conservatives themselves sometimes read texts differently—for instance, in the case of the Genesis 19 story of Sodom and Gomorrah. Robert Gagnon in *The Bible and Homosexual Practice: Texts and Hermeneutics* defends the traditional interpretation, while Richard Hays in his book *The Moral Vision of the New Testament* writes: "There is nothing in the passage pertinent to a judgment about the morality of consensual homosexual intercourse."[119]

Further, traditionalists argue that reading the whole text and searching for the author's intent is an important part of the work of interpretation. The interpreter has a moral obligation to seek out the meaning of the text.[120]

They suggest that Jesus interprets scripture by evaluating the perspectives of a text from the Torah according to the way it reflects God's vision in creation, along with the possible provision for human hardness of heart. They then have a very important couple of paragraphs, which I think are essential in unpacking the case against the blessing of same-sex relationships. They write:

> *Might same-sex relationships go back to God's creation intent and have the same theological and ethical status as heterosexual relationships? This would fit with the fact that such relationships seem as "natural" to some people as heterosexual relationships seem to other people, yet it can hardly be reckoned to fit with the Torah's own vision of creation and of what is "natural" in the way that is the case with a forswearing of anger, lust, swearing oaths, and forgoing revenge. Jesus points out that the opening chapters of the Torah describe God making humanity male and female and describe a man leaving his parents to be joined to a woman. It is hard to see how this could fit with the idea that a same-sex marriage is just as valid a creation reality as a heterosexual marriage.*

> *The argument is often made that the scriptural treatment of chattel slavery, the subordination of women, and the prohibition of usury are moral issues where subsequent reflection and experience led to genuine change in the Church's teaching, and that the question of same-sex relationships poses the same kind of challenge to accept the wisdom of a new perspective. However, this comparison really does not work. With regard to the subordination of women, it is explicit in Genesis 3 that men's ruling over women came about as result of human disobedience rather than as an original intention of creation. Texts that require the subordination of women can therefore plausibly be seen as concessions to human sinfulness, and reflect the disorder of humanity after the fall.*

> *The same description in Genesis 1:27 of humanity made in God's image in turn leads to a description of humanity's vocation to cultivate and tend the garden; there is no hint of slavery or servitude in human relationships. Texts in the Torah that later regularize servitude are concerned to constrain an institution that exists because of the fallenness of humankind. The New Testament has been seen as more acquiescent to slavery, but there are texts (e.g., 1 Tim 1:10) that put human trafficking in a negative light. We should regard the apparent acquiescence (not at all the same as approval, by the way!) as largely a reflection of the immense power and apparent resistance to change of the political and legal institutions of the Roman Empire within which the Church had to manage.*

> *There are no indications in Scripture parallel to the principles used against slavery, racism and the subordination of women to which we could appeal to demonstrate that God's creation ideal should also embrace same-sex relationships. Rather, the portrayal of human origins in Genesis points in the opposite direction. There, the centerpiece in the vision of human marriage is not intimacy or relationship or*

romance but family. The man and the woman will be the means and the context in which the family will grow in such a way as to serve God and serve the land. This point in itself does not exclude same-sex marriages, but it does suggest they are not an equally valid option.

If the Church—or at least a large portion of it in western countries—does actually move ahead on the question of accepting same-sex relationships, it may appear to be following a pattern of moral change demonstrated in the past. In our judgment, however, the reasoning behind this change in viewing marriage and sexual relations will have come more from assimilation to modern culture than from following Jesus in learning how better to understand and live by the Scriptures."[121]

The text presented continues in the report with a section on scriptural portions important to the argument of upholding traditional marriage, then a discussion on natural law, followed by theological trends and concerns about abuses within the Church towards gay and lesbian people. They also finish with a reflection on the nature of mission from a traditionalist perspective and how to engage in a thoughtful and disciplined way of creating space for gay and lesbian people within a Christian community.

I did find their closing remarks important and worth inserting. Here they are:

We need to put into proper perspective the inflated importance we naturally attach to sexual fulfillment and even marriage. We have the teaching of Jesus about the disappearance of marriage and family relationships in the kingdom of heaven, and we have the examples and teaching of both Jesus and Paul, who made clear that physical sexual needs, expressions, and relationships are temporary and secondary compared to our destiny as co-heirs with Christ. "The goal for homosexual and heterosexual alike is fulfillment and wholeness in Christ." Recovery and proclamation of that conviction is the challenge for our Church.[122]

I am not intending to cut this short as I think the full argument makes a much better case for itself and I would encourage you to read it regardless of your position. I do think in this section I have included for you how the traditionalist or conservative argument makes its case against same-sex relationships based on scripture—how they argue for a theological bulwark to culture. Yet at the same time I believe I have shown that they, too, are committed to trying to figure out how individuals reflect the Christlike wholeness Christians manifest in their life.

The Liberal View on Same-Sex Blessings

While the conservative argument takes Richard Hooker, natural law, scripture, science and mission as their outline, the liberals take a completely different approach. They begin with mission, scripture, the vows, and the patristic witness for marital themes on relationships and then return to mission.

The liberals make the case that, rather than being revisionist or doing something purely that is new, they are expanding something that is old. They take for themselves then the name of "expansionists." I take this to mean they are expanding the notion that people in same-sex relationships can have their commitment to one another blessed by the church.

They argue that marriage itself is a discipline and a way in which sinners receive grace. The vows, they argue, are ways in which two people come together as sinners, recognizing their dependence upon one another and upon God.[123] They argue that in doing this the blessing of a same-sex couple's covenant relationship can be seen as an icon of Christ's love for the world and church.

They believe that the Church should marry same-sex couples because it requires a testimony of love and recognizes their own need for sanctification as individuals. The grace and marital virtues that the Church offers to heterosexual couples would improve the Christian lives of the gay and lesbian couples as well. Furthermore, they argue that this is, in fact, the mission of the Church: to offer grace to sinful people and inspire virtue through a covenant with one another and with God. The marriage rite itself, the blessing, places couples into a discipline of life lived one to another and Christ. In doing so they believe this rite can be an image of how God is reconciling the world to himself (2 Cor 5:19). They write:

> *This is not so much a new theology of marriage… We base our argument, then, not on autonomy, individualism, or personal experience, but on the embodied discipline—that of marriage—by which God may transform longing into charity and dispositions to love into works of virtue. Can we credit what we pray in the marriage rite, that God may "make their life together a sign of Christ's love to this sinful and broken world, that unity may overcome estrangement, forgiveness heal guilt, and joy conquer despair." (BCP, 429)*[124]

Not unlike the conservative view they also go to Augustine, which I find interesting. They continue with this statement:

> *Because Scripture demands to be interpreted in accord with the mission of God, we*

should not so confine it to any one sense, as to expose the faith to ridicule (Augustine, Confessions V.5, De Genesi ad litteram 1; Aquinas, De potentia 4, 1, r). For different mission partners will inevitably ridicule the faith in some way, causing the church to see different aspects of the truth that God desires holiness. This view of Scripture is the view of Augustine: that God gives us the difficult work of interpreting Scripture in order to make finite, sin-darkened readers capable of growing into the truth. Scripture gives itself to many readings that its readers may slowly learn to orient their desire to God's desire for them.

I want to take another excerpt where the use of scripture in the liberal, or expansionist view, helps us to clearly see the difference by which the two groups come to read the scripture.

Alongside the marriage practices described in Scripture, even in their variety, our proposal that the Church extend marriage to same-sex couples appears transgressive. Yet, within the testimony of the early church's way of reading Scripture, it appears to fit the Spirit of adoption (Rom 8:15, 23) that exceeds Paul's expectation by grafting wild branches onto the domestic olive (Rom 11:24). Acts portrays the apostles and the earliest church as following the presence of the Spirit even when the Spirit's activity seemed to exceed the plain sense of Scripture. In Romans and Galatians, Paul must defend the astonishing inclusion of Gentiles, which exceeded theological assumptions, and elaborate the coherence of a way of life that ran against moral assumptions. We argue here, that analogously, marrying same-sex couples comports with the mission of God celebrated by the Spirit in the body of Christ, even though it seems to exceed the marriage practices assumed by Scripture and honored by tradition.

...We do not claim that biblical writers imagined or anticipated marriages of two women or two men. The New Testament does, however, give evidence that the followers of Jesus and the churches begun by Paul and other missionaries took a skeptical perspective on both male-female marriage and the patriarchal family. In Mark, Jesus makes the true mark of a sibling and kindred relationship doing the will of God (Mk. 3:31-35). Paul's letters show that both he and some members of the churches understood baptism into Christ to commend celibacy (1 Cor 7). Many texts in the gospels and letters attest to the ascetic character of these early communities. Later Christian writers then reasserted the primacy of marriage and the household as the model for the shape of the church. Marriage practices supported by the early church therefore hold in tension both those who radically relativize the traditional family in preference for celibacy or "spiritual" family and those that make the traditional family, what we would call today the "biological family" the sole Christian model. Our approach combines the two New Testament values of

asceticism and household: marriage is a school for virtue, a household asceticism: "for better for worse," "forsaking all others" (Book of Common Prayer 427, 424).

The history of interpreting these diverse texts has yielded various kinds of support for sex relations, sexual understanding, and marital practice. In different periods and with distinctive priorities they have celebrated the superiority of celibacy and the vocation of Christian marriage, promoted a celibate male priesthood and a married clergy, restricted ordination to males and lately extended it to women. Guided by the reading of Scripture in the prayers and blessing of marriage in the Book of Common Prayer, we argue that faithful marriage partnership can also be the aspiration of same-sex couples just as it is for opposite-sex couples. Adapted to include partners of the same sex, Christian marriage still retains procreation as one of its purposes (BCP, 423). Marriage creates a family and a home for the nurture of children. Beyond the good of procreation, marriage makes the conditions for companionship and friendship that God intends both for mutual joy and for the sanctification and maturation of the individuals within it. We testify that in this, God shows no partiality. Opposite-sex as well as same-sex couples who engage in this covenant undertake extraordinary promises in the face of great odds and with God's help make a vivid witness to the gospel of Jesus Christ and the church established in his name.

"It has seemed good to the that they should marry" (Acts 15:28). Reading Scripture for the way marriage bears witness to God seems to depend at least in part on how a reading community understands the mission of God in its context. We read in the community that the Spirit makes. Because the Spirit spans the centuries, our argument reads Scripture in the company of patristic interpreters as well as in the company of readers long silenced by the tradition.

Key to this argument is that Paul himself loosened the requirements of scripture as the emerging early Christian movement was growing. The liberals or expansionists argue that, in fact, there were many instances where Paul did this despite the clarity with which the scripture implicitly restricted believers. We might remember our earlier discourse about dietary laws and we would want to add to it circumcision. This is an important and essential piece of the expansionist argument. It is key for what they are saying—as the mission of Christ is pursued, there are times when, despite the words of scripture, a faithful church may choose to loosen binding prohibitions for the sake of those being added to the number of faithful Christians.

The liberal or expansionist argument holds that the Church learns how to interpret scripture by being the Body of Christ. The report says:

[The church] learns the truth of Scripture by living from marriage to its Bridegroom, and therefore not from self-sufficiency but from self-donation to another. That means that the church reads Scripture not in purity but from mission, a mission that must leave it changed. The church takes part in the mission of the Trinity when she goes out from the Father in the person of the Son and in the community of the Spirit. She evangelizes others and herself by going out of herself and receiving into herself those who are different, as the Son and Spirit do in their missions.

The liberal argument then goes through the marriage service itself and takes each vow and illustrates how it is a vow to all sinners wishing to live in lives of covenant with one another and with God. They then continue to make their case that the expansion of the marriage rite for the Church will reveal more who Christ is in relationship to humanity and specifically his Church.

As I did with the conservative/traditional argument, I want to include their concluding statement in this synopsis and overview with a quote from the liberal/expansionist paper.

We do not call for an end to disagreement, for that is part of the labor of our common baptism into God's mission. The Father sent the Son and the Spirit into a finite and fallen world where only diversity could image infinity and only history could reconcile them. Baptism prepares human beings for this arduous process by binding them together, and promises them that contrary to human expectations, their disagreement will have been for blessing: "thou preparest a table for me in the presence of mine enemies" (Ps 23:5). Under conditions of both diversity and division, disagreement can become a Spirit-given way of discerning the form of the Son. Baptism binds us together for the long process of making the body of Christ whole and complete in all its members. We are baptized into the Father, the Son, and the Spirit so that we can better disagree. The bonds of baptism tell us that there is no salvation without the others and require therefore the greatest freedom for disagreement rather than the narrowest slice of purity.

The Supreme Court and General Convention 78

June 27, 2015, the Supreme Court of the United States ruled that the legal right to marry was protected for all Americans. This ruling became public while the Episcopal Church was meeting at the 78th General Convention. At this convention the Episcopal Church approved, as imagined when I first wrote *Unity in Mission*, new liturgical rites that expand marriage. The rites allow for the continued marriage rite for a man and a woman and expand the offerings of liturgies for same-sex couples.

The report of the Task Force to Study Marriage offered that marriage, all marriage, is a Christian vocation. The work of all those who are married is to reflect the "eternal union of Christ and the Church."[125] They offer that marriage is a reflection of "Christ is all in all" from Colossians 3:11.[126] Marriage is a vocation that models and reveals, through a "lifelong communal call to abide and grow," God's ultimate beckoning that we all come into his saving embrace.[127]

The essay on the Biblical and Theological Framework found in the Task Force on Marriage report goes through the theological changes found in scripture on marriage. They remind us of statements made previously in this paper that there is trajectory of understanding about marriage with many variations. They offer that our own Anglican theology is that we wrestle with the scripture and seek to understand its "sufficiency of the Holy Scriptures for salvation" (Article VI). They write:

> *The concept is that not every theological issue need be addressed in detail, and that a set of basic guiding principles can set the ground rules within which the Church has authority to act. The Creeds, of course, say nothing of matrimony; moreover, the classical Anglican catechisms are also silent on it, while the 1979 BCP catechism gives only a brief description of it on page 861. The Articles of Religion decline to name matrimony a sacrament (as it "lacks any visible sign or ceremony ordained of God"), and classify it as an estate allowed (Article XXV), while holding it to be available to clergy (as to all Christians) as they judge it to be conducive to a moral life (Article XXXII). Given the relatively sparse attention given to marriage, the principal doctrinal formularies of the early Church and later Anglicanism, we are left with what the Scripture and the liturgies of the Church tell us about it.[128]*

They also point out that Cranmer and succeeding rites of marriage moved us beyond a mere contractual obligation towards the mutual commitment of the couple. The marriage rite is about the commitment of individuals to another—to the other. The commitment seeks the transformation of life lived in a commitment to another. It is this commitment by the couple that is the center of the rite.

The blessing of the Church comes from the witness made by the gathered community. The authors write, "'From this day forward' the couple 'takes' each other, creating a new reality in their union as one in heart, body, and mind. It is this relationship that has been imbued with the Holy Spirit through prayer and blessing in the Name of God, which points to what makes a marriage holy."[129]

The expansion of the marriage rite was approved by the wider Episcopal Church at its 78th meeting.

Their goal was not to undo the nature of marriage between a man and a woman but instead to broaden and expand it to include same-sex relationships so that people might live together a life of fidelity for the purpose of revealing to the world what we hold as true in Paul's letter to the Philippians 2.6 might be revealed.

> Christ Jesus,
> 6 who, though he was in the form of God,
>   did not regard equality with God
>   as something to be exploited,
> 7 but emptied himself,
>   taking the form of a slave,
>   being born in human likeness.
> And being found in human form,
> 8 he humbled himself
>   and became obedient to the point of death—
>   even death on a cross.
> 9 Therefore God also highly exalted him
>   and gave him the name
>   that is above every name,
> 10 so that at the name of Jesus
>   every knee should bend,
>   in heaven and on earth and under the earth,
> 11 and every tongue should confess
>   that Jesus Christ is Lord,
>   to the glory of God the Father.

Note their statement, at the 78th General Convention, regarding the approved canon and liturgy did not change the doctrine of marriage. It offered a canon change that would allow room for individuals to be protected in signing legal marriage licenses for the state. They wanted to provide space for both dissenting theology and pastoral room for those wishing to expand marriage. In a statement by The Rt. Rev. Tom Ely in presenting the proposals they were clear, "The focus is on God's unconditional faithfulness and forgiveness; the paradox of union and difference in Christ; and Christ's self-offering love that is at the heart of the Paschal Mystery."

Some Thoughts

I strongly encourage those of you interested in these views to read both articles with care. I find that they are very different and run almost on different rails of the Anglican tradition. You may also wish to read the report to General Convention 78 entitled The Report of the Task Force on the Study Marriage.[130]

As I have shown in the brief synopsis (which does not do justice to either paper), the two cases use two completely different methods for different purposes. I did this because, after being in this discussion for the whole life of my ministry, I see that we have reached a point in which the two divergent sides will not meet in the middle. Truly there will be people who resonate with bits of each argument; we don't all think in monolithic terms. Our experience of life itself and our own story will find in each argument the parts that speak to us. Within the church politic, though, there is a divide.

On the one hand, "The conservative paper argues that accepting same-sex marriage contradicts moral teachings of Scripture and the guidance of reason by natural law. It therefore defends readings of Scripture that support traditional heterosexual marriage … It supports those readings with natural law principles of sexual complementarity and procreative purpose in marriage." On the other hand, the liberal paper "does not reason from specific social [I would say moral] teachings but from the moral patterns of Scripture." Their argument does not "defeat biblical suspicions of various sexual relations." The liberal argument does attempt to illustrate "how God uses marital faithfulness to heal and perfect sinners."

I believe the lay reader of these two texts, along with the skilled academician, sees that, regardless of how one takes up the argument and seeks to make their case, there are profound effects on our current theological thinking both within The Episcopal Church and the global Anglican Communion. They demonstrate the burden that an expansion of marriage must bear within the Anglican Communion. I believe both papers do well in their acknowledgement of our U.S. and Western culture and how our struggle challenges good Christian people here and abroad. I also fear that the two papers do not particularly bring the two differing sides together.

There is no great dialectic here. I rather find there are two separate conversations. There is in these two conversations, two completely different and competing theologies.

It is very much up to the reader to examine the texts and try and find a convergence within one's own heart, or even simply to find a place upon which to stand.

I think the great benefit of reading both papers is the well-done Anglican thought that illuminates for the churchgoer the complexities and yet true gift our Anglican theology has to offer when making a case for or against the blessing of same-sex couples. I also think it is a clarion bell ringing out the reality that we are simply stuck with two good and competing cases for the truth.

Following the vote approving same-sex marriage in the House of Bishops a group of traditionalist bishops offered a statement as a minority report. I believe it reveals the conflict on same-sec marriage and where it stands today. It was signed by 16 active bishops of The Episcopal Church. They wrote:

> *As bishops of the Church, we must dissent from these actions.*
>
> *We affirm Minority Report #1, which was appended to the text of Resolution A036:*
>
> *The nature, purpose, and meaning of marriage, as traditionally understood by Christians, are summed up in the words of the Book of Common Prayer:*
>
> *"The bond and covenant of marriage was established by God in creation, and our Lord Jesus Christ adorned this manner of life by his presence and first miracle at a wedding in Cana of Galilee. It signifies to us the mystery of the union between Christ and his Church, and Holy Scripture commends it to be honored by all people.*
>
> *The union of husband and wife in heart, body, and mind is intended by God for their mutual joy; for the help and comfort given one another in prosperity and adversity; and, when it is God's will, for the procreation of children and their nurture in the knowledge and love of the Lord" (BCP, p. 423) The nature, purpose, and meaning of marriage are linked to the relationship of man and woman. The promises and vows of marriage presuppose husband and wife as the partners who are made one flesh in marriage. This understanding is a reasonable one, as well as in accord with Holy Scripture and Christian tradition in their teaching about marriage.*
>
> *When we were ordained as bishops in the one, holy, catholic, and apostolic Church, we vowed to "guard the faith, unity, and discipline of the Church of God" (BCP, p. 518). We renew that promise; and in light of the actions of General Convention, and of our own deep pastoral and theological convictions, we pledge ourselves to "Maintain the unity of the Spirit in the bond of peace" (Eph. 4:3). The bonds created in baptism are indissoluble, and we share one bread and one cup in the Eucharist. We are committed to the Church and its people, even in the midst of painful disagreement.*
>
> *"Speak the truth in love" (Eph. 4:15). When we disagree with the Church's actions, we will do so openly and transparently and – with the Spirit's help – charitably. We are grateful that Resolution A054 includes provision for bishops*

and priests to exercise their conscience; but we realize at the same time that we have entered a season in which the tensions over these difficult matters may grow. We pray for the grace to be clear about our convictions and, at the same time, to love brothers and sisters with whom we disagree.

"Welcome one another . . . just as Christ has welcomed [us]" (Rom. 15:7). Our commitment to the Church includes a commitment to our gay and lesbian brothers and sisters. We will walk with them, pray with and for them, and seek ways to engage in pastoral conversation. We rejoice that Jesus' embrace includes all of us.

We are mindful that the decisions of the 78th General Convention do not take place in isolation. The Episcopal Church is part of a larger whole, the Anglican Communion. We remain committed to that Communion and to the historic See of Canterbury, and we will continue to honor the three moratoria requested in the Windsor Report and affirmed by the Instruments of Communion.

We invite bishops and any Episcopalians who share these commitments to join us in this statement, and to affirm with us our love for our Lord Jesus Christ, our commitment to The Episcopal Church, and the Anglican Communion, and our dissent from these actions.

I believe here highlighted are marks of *Unity in Mission*. They are clear about their theological position of a natural law understanding of the scripture (as proposed above). They also though go on to be clear that they will speak truthfully to their brothers and sisters even though they are a minority. Furthermore, they commit to the remaining faithful members of The Episcopal Church. Quoting Ephesians 4.3 they promise to "'Maintain the unity of the Spirit in the bond of peace' (Eph. 4:3). The bonds created in baptism are indissoluble, and we share one bread and one cup in the Eucharist. We are committed to the Church and its people, even in the midst of painful disagreement." The traditionalist bishops commit themselves to continuing ministry inline with their conscience but at the same time making pastoral room for caring for the GLBT communities in their own dioceses.

The same-sex marriage resolutions that were passed did not change the theology of our church regarding heterosexual marriage as the changes were not made to The Book of Common Prayer. Just as in 2011 I explained that in 2015 the church would in fact approve same-sex marriage rites, I am also very clear that in either 2018 or 2021 The Episcopal Church General Convention will formally adopt liturgies expanding the marriage canon to include same-sex couples. This will not undo the theology rooted in heterosexual marriage. It will expand our theological language to include marriage for same-sex couples.

At General Convention in 2015 the resolutions were clear though that clergy could not be forced to do same-sex marriages. Bishops could not be forced to allow same-sex marriages in their own dioceses. In this way the resolutions themselves offered the ability for The Episcopal Church to remain unified in mission despite its deep differences on marriage.

The House of Bishops did something unique in response to the traditionalist "minority statement." The House of Bishops reached out affirming our unity in mission despite our differences. The statement adopted by the House reads:

We the House of Bishops of The Episcopal Church wish to express our love and appreciation to our colleagues who identify as Communion Partners and those bishops who have affinity with the Communion Partners' position as stated in their "Communion Partners Salt Lake City Statement." Our time together in Salt Lake City, in conversation and in prayer, has demonstrated how profoundly the love of God in Jesus binds us together and empowers us for service to God's mission. As we have waited upon the leading of the Holy Spirit in our deliberations, we have been reminded that the House of Bishops is richly gifted with many voices and perspectives on matters of theological, liturgical, and pastoral significance. This has been shown in our discernment with respect to doctrinal matters relative to Christian marriage. We thank God for the rich variety of voices in our House, in our dioceses, in The Episcopal Church, and in the Anglican Communion, that reflect the wideness of God's mercy and presence in the Church and in the world.

We give particular thanks for the steadfast witness of our colleagues in the Communion Partners. We value and rely on their commitment to The Episcopal Church and the Anglican Communion. We recognize that theirs is a minority voice in the House of Bishops in our deliberations with respect to Christian marriage; and we affirm that despite our differences they are an indispensable part of who we are as the House of Bishops of The Episcopal Church. Our church needs their witness. Further, we appreciate that each of us will return to dioceses where there will be a variety of responses to Resolutions A054 and A036. The equanimity, generosity, and graciousness with which the Communion Partners have shared their views on Christian marriage and remain in relationship is a model for us and for the lay and ordained leaders in our dioceses to follow. We thank God that in the fullness of the Holy Trinity we can and must remain together as the Body of Christ in our dioceses, in The Episcopal Church, and in our relationships with sisters and brothers in Christ in the Anglican Communion. The bonds created in baptism are indeed indissoluble and we pray that we have the confidence to rely upon the Holy Spirit who will continue to hold us all together as partners in communion through the love of God in Jesus.

The House of Bishops recognize that it is a community more

complicated than the minority statement makes it sound. Many in the House of Bishops offered that they believe strongly in the theology of heterosexual marriage but that they believed pastorally and for deep convictions this theology must be broadened (not to get rid of marriage) to create marriage for those same-sex couples who wish to life in a covenanted rule of life marked with fidelity and monogamy.

The Mind of the House Statement also affirmed that the House itself is a diverse community but that it is committed to reflect the life of the Holy Trinity and remain unified in mission despite their uniformity on marriage. The House of Bishops made clear their commitment to all Episcopalians and members of the worldwide Anglican Communion. They pledged to work hard to mend the bods of affection based upon the baptismal grace give by the Holy Spirit that all who follow Jesus may be one.

Historians of the community of bishops in The Episcopal Church recognize that this was historic. It was historic that the minority and majority should treat one another with dignity and respect in all deliberations. It was historic in that there was abundant room made for broad disagreement. There was an Anglican comprehensiveness expressed and legislated that was remarkable. Many stated in conversation one to another within the House of Bishops that it was in a different place – a more mature place.

I imagine that most conflicts of such a divided nature always run a set of complicated tracks, crossing and re-crossing one another as they make their way through time and prayer. Division finds peace, peace allows for difference, difference makes room for unity beyond uniformity. This is of course not new in Christian history. A close reading of texts from the first centuries of our Church illustrates the great divisions on theology, ecclesiology and missiology. Theological battles and conflicts were violent and costly in terms of human life. The Christian Church was literally at war with itself.

In the midst of any given time period, these competing thoughts also seem to stand in complete opposition to one another. A reading of the Donald K. McKim's seminal book *Theological Turning Points: Major Issues in Christian Thought* shows the depth by which competing views in our history have always seemed to run on parallel tracks until the Church reconciles itself to Christ. This can take centuries, and in some cases the great theological controversies and their themes continue to be wrestled out through prayerful discernment and discussion even to this day. McKim writes:

Christian theology has come a long way, zigging and zagging from its earliest days through many expressions of faith. The path has not always been smooth or straight. Through theological debate and dialogue new forms of expression arise and new answers are given to old questions. Yet new answers inevitably raise new questions, and so it goes.

The Christian church and Christian theology can only turn new corners, however, when critical and sustained attention is given to all the issues raised by adherents. While the main figures in the history of theology are often considered "superstars," theology at its best is done through the open participation of people in all arenas and cultures, so that what results can resonate with truth and touch the lives of people in many contexts. As theology today becomes open to more and more people with varying accents and experiences, the tapestry of Christianity can be increasingly enriched. New contexts, methods, issues, and conclusions will come. New turning points will arise, and from these new resources the continuing history of Christian doctrine will emerge.[131]

I believe we are in the midst of just such a struggle. It is perhaps a struggle that will continue long after our part in its conversation is long since played out and we will have entered into nearer company with God, Christ Jesus and through the power of the Holy Spirit, the saints in light. Nevertheless, you and I must find a Christian unity beyond this difference and continue our missionary work of proclaiming the Gospel in spite of our difference and the gulf that appears before our beloved Church.

8 A COMMUNAL RESPONSE

How we are to respond to one another in the midst of this divide? An answer comes from an essential ingredient to life at our very own Seminary of the Southwest. I believe their "Conversation Covenant" offers a way in which we may choose to be in community together.[132]

The Very Rev. Doug Travis says this about the Covenant, "One way we express our Christian friendship is through our 'Conversation Covenant,' which is rooted in the baptismal covenant. We seek to listen as well as speak, to show kindness and humility, and to acknowledge that we might be wrong. We yearn to be a people who without exception see in the face of the 'other,' a friend, someone for whom Jesus has died and whom Jesus has invited to join him at his table, the heavenly banquet."

We, the people of the Episcopal Church and the Anglican Communion, have an opportunity to continue the great tradition of this diocese in forging a way through division and becoming Christian friends. It is a characteristic that has shaped and formed us from our very beginning. It is the recognition in one another of a fellow pilgrim, sinner and neighbor who, through the grace of God and his crucifixion and resurrection, is our brother and sister.

It is my belief that the Church is busy at work interpreting the Gospel of Good News to the world and seeking to inquire how we might better live out our Christian faith. We do this in word and we do this in deed. Such reflection is not a private affair but is lived out, and our lives become icons of this engagement with scripture, with God, and with the Christian community. People look at us and they see the kind of Christian we are—based upon our expressions of love to one another and to our neighbor.

In such a community, made up of individuals willing to journey together, "frank, confident, and trustful conversation" is the hallmark of Christ's love in our midst.[121] Such conversation is an essential ingredient for our common and communal transformation. We cannot shy away from the other and their perspective. Christian conversation is always and everywhere best shaped by reading the whole text—even the parts with which we disagree. It is engaging in conversation with individuals, even those who have a different perspective.

At times in Christian history such as these, we face hard topics and we know that such conversations are difficult, most especially when we dare to speak with someone who disagrees with us. These conversations can be "difficult, even disturbing," because often times our assumptions are challenged.[133] Our hopes that we will never see the passage of rites for blessing a same-sex couple, or our hope that they will be available soon, come into direct conflict with other people's ideas about how things are to be. Our "opinions and certainties" are challenged by those who see the world differently or interpret a text differently. Yet these moments are often powerful moments of formation in the Christian faith. These conversations are landmarks along our pilgrim journey.

It is true that walking apart can seem easier to some than doing the difficult work of listening to the other. It is true that at times cultural war seems the only way forward. Fight or flight is symptomatic of a life that does not embrace our Anglican identity and leaves the mission of the Church subservient to forces of division and darkness. It is destructive and we are good people who wish to do nothing more than find our way into the bosom of the God who loves us. We are a good people who wish to do good works and minister well. We want to be faithful and we want to follow Jesus.

In order for us to move forward and into a life lived in the midst of this conflict, we must begin by acknowledging that we are all made in the image of God and must, therefore, treat one another with respect and dignity.[134] We must do this for those with whom we agree and we must do this for those with whom we disagree. We must not repay evil for evil and we must seek to be at peace with our brothers and sisters.

In order for us to live in the midst of these conflicting ideas, we must give ourselves—and our neighbor—freedom to explore different ideas and beliefs as well as to grow and to change theologically.[135] None of us has been birthed into this world fully formed. Many of us do not fully understand the depth to which this division runs in our Church. Many of us do not even understand the full scriptural meaning of the texts upon which our ideas may be grounded. We must seek out resources, learn, and try to understand the complexity of this issue. Despite what our culture teaches us, researching on Wikipedia does not make us an expert.

Not only do we need space but we need to remember our sinfulness.

"We share a common sinfulness and, therefore, will understand only partially and be mistaken frequently," the Conversation Covenant says. Even Saint Paul said in 1 Corinthians 13:12, "Now we see but a poor reflection as in a mirror; then we shall see face to face. Now I know in part; then I shall know fully, even as I am fully known."

In order to live together in the midst of this conflict, we must reject the prevailing cultural notion that we should be with only those who are like-minded. Christianity and our Anglican tradition tell us clearly that we do not have to agree in order to love one another. I grew up in this diocese and I have seen the power of redeeming love that is present in this Church. I know many of you by name and I know many who now stand on the opposite side of the theological fence from one another. I believe that it wounds God when we allow our disagreements to keep us from loving one another as Christ has loved us.

We have to be clear that "our conversations, even our most passionate disagreements, take place in the Spirit whom we seek not to grieve."[136] In doing so, we must realize that our enterprise of community and communion is a sacramental and grace-filled gift of the Holy Spirit. We are Christ's own gift to one another, and that gift was purchased for us on the cross that we might all be drawn ever closer together and ever closer to God.

When we begin from this perspective, we may approach the conversation with a willingness to listen and learn, acknowledging the value of opposing views. We can treat one another as honest inquirers, attempting to discern God's truth in a complex world, and we give ourselves permission to engage ideas without attacking or dismissing those who hold them. We are able to consider the possibility that we might be mistaken, secure in the knowledge of the love and forgiveness we have all received in Christ. We are able, no matter how difficult the subject, to challenge one another while seeking not to give offense. We seek, therefore, to acknowledge stereotypes, ask for clarification in order to avoid misunderstandings, and make room for complexity.

The nuptial mystery, in which two who are profoundly different become one, makes our unity in the face of conflict especially profound. In the creation narrative of Genesis, we see the dissolution of two who were intended to support each other. But towards the conclusion of the Revelation of St. John, as the Holy Jerusalem descends from heaven to earth adorned as a bride prepared for her bridegroom, we see the reconciliation and reunion of heaven and earth, which implies the reconciliation and reunion of those who had been separated to become one. Because the Church is an icon of the way God has made one all things that are in heaven and in earth, and because the Church expresses this iconographic union, we are encouraged to find our way forward together.

It is my belief that God has called us together. We are given as family to one another and we are offered a sacred moment, this moment of deep conflict and divide, in which to show our commitment to God by committing ourselves to one another. I believe that we--the people of the Diocese of Texas--have it within ourselves to choose to walk humbly with God and with one another, to remain united in mission despite our disagreements, and to treat one another with respect and dignity. In so doing, you and I together, will light a fire of reconciliation and mission for all the world to see. We shall together make our witness of the hope that is in us—the good news of salvation. We shall sit and eat at the table together. We will, as the people of the Diocese of Texas, become ourselves an icon of the nuptial mystery of God's reconciling action of uniting heaven to earth and earth to heaven.

A second vision of our response comes to us through the work of the Community of the Cross of Nails from Coventry Cathedral. Following a night of heavy bombing during the Coventry Blitz during World War II, a stonemason, Jock Forbes, saw two wooden beams lying in the shape of a cross and tied them together. On the day following the bombing, the Dean began to speak of reconciliation and forgiveness. Here is made Coventry Cathedral as a witness to the essential work of God that is reconciliation. The Community of the Cross of Nails became a global society that seeks to undertake, in a very real way, the work of reconciliation.

We find here too, our present Archbishop of Canterbury's own understanding of the Church's work. "Reconciliation doesn't mean we all agree," said the Most Rev. and Rt. Hon. Justin Welby says of this ministry. "It means we find ways of disagreeing—perhaps very passionately—but loving each other deeply at the same time, and being deeply committed to each other. That's the challenge for the church if we are actually going to speak to our society, which is increasingly divided in many different ways."[137]

The work of Canon David Porter and the Very Rev. John Witcombe (Dean of Coventry Cathedral) has helped me to understand that we are a people at work in the world. We bear witness to God's work and our own to heal history, to build a commons of peace and catholicity, where we can celebrate even though we live with differences of opinion. This is a moment to claim our work and expand that peaceful and peace-filled commons out in the world.

What shall be the church's witness in the midst of great division on marriage? I believe and call us to be in conversation and seek to be witnesses first and foremost of reconciliation.

9 A STRATEGY FOR UNITY IN MISSION

Since 2011, the Diocese of Texas has sought to be a witness of unity in mission despite our deep divisions. Our work has been used globally to build a foundation for discussion about how our churches (local and provincial) stay together in the midst of great change. Same-sex marriage is not going to be the last issue that will divide us, just as it is not the first. Our opportunity as a wider family of provinces and as a Communion as a whole is to be witness of God's reconciling ministry through deep conversations.

This strategy is not that complicated: stay together to share the Good News of Salvation and how we are saved through God in Christ Jesus. And stay together that we might serve our community and be neighbor to them. In doing this we shall be known as disciples of Jesus and we shall be at work changing the world. To stay together we must live with our difference. We must honor our diverse opinions. To stay together we must live and work together hand in hand. As the old folk song based upon John 13:35 is clear. The words are:

> We are one in the Spirit
> We are one in the Lord
> We are one in the Spirit
> We are one in the Lord
> And we pray that all unity may one day be restored
> And they'll know we are Christians by our love, by our love
> Yes, they'll know we are Christians by our love
> We will work with each other
> We will work side by side
> We will work with each other
> We will work side by side

And we'll guard each man's dignity and save each man's pride
And they'll know we are Christians by our love, by our love. [138]

Our unity is more than simply going along to get along: it is itself evangelism about the God of love who unites heaven and earth. The strategy actually demands that those who participate hold one another's views as sincere. It requires that we believe that all have the very best faithful intentions. In Texas this has meant that leadership truly makes room for the diverse opinions and invites all to the table together to work for the sake of the Gospel.

There are echoes of these desires throughout Communion documents. Thirty-five leaders of the global church, called primates, were clear that while we are divided theologically we all make our witness to the dignity of human beings. They wrote in a statement following their meeting that they understood the importance first of unity in mission as a wider communion. Secondly, they understood the importance of pastoral care and work with the LGBT community. Moreover, they also offered clarity that we seek to protect and guard the dignity of our LGBT community.

They stated clearly, "We also wish to make it quite clear that in our discussion and assessment of the moral appropriateness of specific human behaviours, we continue unreservedly to be committed to the pastoral support and care of homosexual people. The victimisation or diminishment of human beings whose affections happen to be ordered towards people of the same sex is anathema to us. We assure homosexual people that they are children of God, loved and valued by him, and deserving of the best we can give of pastoral care and friendship."[139]

They concluded their communication with these words:

> *Indeed, in the course of our meeting, we have become even more mindful of the indissoluble link between Christian unity and Christian mission, as this is expressed in Jesus' own prayer that his disciples should be one that the world may believe (John 17.21). Accordingly, we pray for the continuing blessing of God's unity and peace as we recommit ourselves to the mission of the Anglican Communion, which we share with the whole people of God, in the transformation of our troubled world.*

Therefore, our work as Anglicans is to stay together in our differences. We must work ever harder to walk together. This will mean not allowing any one action of any one group to keep us from sitting at the table together. After the 78th General Convention in 2015 the Archbishop of

Canterbury Justin Welby spoke of the importance of remaining together and being focused on mission:

> *At a time of such suffering around the world, he stated that this was a moment for the church to be looking outwards. We continue to mourn with all those who are grieving loved ones and caring for the injured from the terrorist attacks in Sousse, Kuwait and Lyons, and from the racist attacks in Charleston.*

Archbishop Welby urges prayer for the life of the Anglican Communion; for a space for the strengthening of the interdependent relationships between provinces, so that in the face of diversity and disagreement, Anglicans may be a force for peace and seek to respond to the Lord Jesus' prayer that "they may be one so that the world may believe" (John 17:21).[140]

The Texas Plan of *Unity in Mission*, as it has come to be known, is an understanding that we will make room within the Diocese of Texas to accept those with different opinions. It allows people to work together despite differences of opinion on the issues of sexuality.

Some churches have gay clergy; others do not. Some churches offer blessings and others do not. Yet all of them serve equally throughout the Diocese together in mission. All of them have found that they can work together to raise up future clergy. We have found a way of accepting one another's orders. We have discovered that we enjoy our company and we are rooted more deeply in God's love for us despite our differences. We have many different parishes with many different leaders.

We are working to build non-shaming conversations and to understand the pain many people feel around the issues of sexuality and marriage. We have stayed together in a time when few have chosen to do so in a society that prides itself on the art of division. Despite the pressure to walk apart fueled by mean spiritedness, which infects many parts of the wider church, we have found conversation with Jesus and are living and working together in a way that has not been seen in a long time. We in the Diocese of Texas recognize this as a gift from God.

Specifically this means that we should gather with as many people as are willing to be present for one another. At a time of great pain or in times of great celebration, the sacred community of God gathers.

The Anglican Communion should gather as primates together for prayer and consultation and mutual support. The Communion should gather for a Lambeth meeting of bishops. We might also consider gathering as an Anglican congress of laity and clergy to celebrate and share our story of mission with one another. We should gather as a global youth movement. We should gather and celebrate the ministry of women in our midst. We should gather because God is the one who gathers us.

In a myriad of possible ways, let us gather as a global communion. We should work fervently to meet and pray, to sing and dance, to listen and to speak the stories of how God is at work in the world bringing peace and justice, serving and protecting the poor, and transforming the world into God's dream for creation. We should gather because God gathers us in that we might go out.

The truth is that the only way to be a reconciling community is to come together.

As a diocese we should chose to walk together. We should rise above the voices to further divide. We should stay together and stay within the Episcopal Church or our own province. We need to allow for and make room for expanding same-sex blessings/marriage for those who wish to live a life of fidelity, but we must also make an extra effort to continue using our traditional marriage rite. We must allow same-sex married clergy to function in churches that wish to call them (should they be approved by the bishop) while at the same time ensuring that congregations that do not wish to call such clergy because of conscience be respected.

We must endeavor to share leadership and support the mission of God through Christ Jesus that is reconciliation. We should walk together out into the world in order to be neighbors to our communities and serve and transform our society into a just and peaceful society. We should work to share the Good News of Salvation. This is our work and this is our song.

As congregations we must do the same. We need to open ourselves up to the difference that is present and begin to focus on the world around us. It is in desperate need of God's dream.

So we should come together.

We should make room to speak our mind and to choose how we wish to go forward. We must see that God has already called us together and that we already live and minister together with difference.

The Diocese of Texas allowed congregations to choose to celebrate or not celebrate the rights of same-sex blessings. Congregations choose the clergy they wish to call into ministry. They do this through a process of discussion and through resolutions at vestry and parish meetings. They choose to stay together and to work together.

Let there be no mistake—we in Texas are not of one mind. But we have intentionally found ways to be clear about our theological identity while at the same time supporting neighbor congregations in their own self-differentiation.

Together we have chosen to work together. Following the Supreme Court's ruling, David Brooks, the *New York Times* columnist, suggested that it is time to put "aside" the culture war oriented around the sexual revolution."[141] Like many, Brooks believes that our arguing has "alienated large parts of three generations from any consideration of religion or belief. Put aside an effort that has been a communications disaster, reducing a rich, complex and beautiful faith into a public obsession with sex. Put aside a culture war that, at least over the near term, you are destined to lose."[142] Instead we should, Brooks believes, become those who help rebuild the "sinews" of society. Our "self-less love," our "faith."[143] We have the opportunity to help people "distinguish between right from wrong."[144] Brooks adequately communicates the reality that we as a united church are the ones who in this time of great change and lack of moral voice can together begin (with the witness of Jesus Christ) offer a path towards a just and loving society.

Living together and working together, given the culture wars around us, will not be without trouble. This will not be easy. It will require that we move towards one another in bonds of peace for the sake of love. It will require resources and the Church should gather such resources necessary and place them at the disposal of a global witness to God's redeeming love.

The work of the Anglican Indaba project is a great project that has brought many together to discover one another's story. Thanks to the Rev. Phil Groves we have a gift in a text and guide to having and holding these conversations. The book is titled *Living Reconciliation.*

We have our challenges. We continue to have differing opinions that threaten our wholeness. Yet, we are given a spiritual exercise for the sake of the Gospel to come together and to meet and to pray. We do this while we are yet far away from one another on many issues. We do this work of unity for the sake of our mission.

By gathering, by coming together, inviting all who would follow Jesus, we walk the middle way together with our diverse opinions on sexuality set aside. I encourage people to prayerfully walk the via media and to honor our Anglican heritage of making new decisions in new contexts for the sake of common mission.

As Hooker wrote, "When the best things are not possible, the best may be made of those that are." Mordecai urged Esther (in chapter four): "You have been chosen for such a time as this." This is our time, our moment to come together for the sake of the one who loved us and died for us that we might be coworkers in the heavenly vineyards of God.

10 ON PILGRIMAGE TOGETHER

We have a faith that is unified and a purposeful mission. We have a desire to work together in sharing the Good News of Salvation and serving our neighbors. We know the very difficult reality of holding our unity while at the same time holding deeply held beliefs. So, we need to practice. One way of practicing is pondering this book and the ideas within. Therefore, what follows is a study guide for Unity in Mission that was prepared for the Diocese of Texas and now expanded here as a way to begin a conversation in your local community.

FOR THE FACILITATOR
Unity in Mission is a rich and engaging work, so this guide assumes that the study group will read the paper outside class over the course of nine meetings. The study guide need not be printed out for the participants, although it could be. Alternately, you may choose simply to create handouts from week to week that include the opening and closing devotions, the getting on board question, and the discussion questions. Additionally, the handout should include the questions for the upcoming session and, if the class is using it, the optional supplementary reading with its questions for that session. (The guide is free and can be found online at http://www.epicenter.org/unity)

Initial publicity for the class could include a handout with a course description, the URL for *Unity in Mission* (unless you decide to print copies) and the discussion questions for the sessions.

THE FORMAT OF EACH SESSION

The format is basically the same for each meeting. Following the time guidelines will complete each session in 45 minutes (or 50 minutes, if you discuss the optional supplementary material). Let's consider each component in turn.

The Approach begins the session with prayer and a silent reflection on a passage of scripture related to the topic. Our hope for the outset of each gathering is to create an opening for the Holy Spirit to be the teacher.

The Getting on Board Question is intended to "break the ice," to help the participants get to know each other and to connect them personally to the subject at hand.

The Introduction may be read aloud by the facilitator or presented in his or her own words, perhaps with additional comments.

The Discussion of the Study Questions forms the heart of the session. You'll find that, in most sessions, we provide more questions than you probably need or will have time to use, so you may select the ones you think most interesting and fruitful. The italicized comments that follow each question are not answers, as you might find in the teacher's edition of a textbook. They simply indicate the direction the authors had in mind when framing this question, and represent their opinions.

THE OPTIONAL SUPPLEMENTARY MATERIAL

Each group may decide whether or not to use this material. If its discussion is to have any hope of staying within the five-minute limit, then the reading needs to be done beforehand outside of class. The optional reading for Session Two provides the only opportunity in this course to examine the new rite of blessing directly. You will need to prepare for this particular class by printing out the liturgies from the General Convention Office website.

The Conclusion brings the session to a close with a suitable scripture reading, free intercessions, the Lord's Prayer and a closing prayer.

LAST THINGS

Just a note on the use of the word "Anglican": Despite the adoption of this term by groups that have separated from The Episcopal Church and use it to distinguish themselves, we use "Anglican" in its traditional sense to mean churches that have their roots in the Church of England and are a part of the Anglican Communion.

You may find the rite and important information about the acts of convention at: http://www.generalconvention.org.

We are very interested to know who might be using this study guide. If you are, then please e-mail the Rev. John Newton at jnewton@epicenter.org. We would welcome your feedback as well.

Preparing this work together has been enjoyable and we hope that "the aim of such instruction" might in some degree be furthered. That aim is the "love that comes from a pure heart, a good conscience, and sincere faith."[145]

Course Plan

Session One
Chapter One by Secretary James Baker III
Preface
Chapter Eight – *A Communal Response*

Session Two
Chapter One – *The Future We Create*

Session Three
Chapter Four – *The Responsibility of the Bishop as Leader*

Session Four
Chapter Five – *Unity as an Instrument of Mission, Part 1*

Session Five
Chapter Five – *Unity as an Instrument of Mission, Part 2*

Session Six
Chapter Six – *Essential Foundations of Marriage, Part 1*

Session Seven
Chapter Four – *Essential Foundations of Marriage, Part 2*

Session Eight
Chapter Seven – *We Are Not of One Mind*

Session Nine
Chapter Nine – *A Strategy for Unity in Mission*

Session One
Preliminaries

I. Introduction—2 minutes

This group study is designed for people interested in reading, pondering and discussing *Unity in Mission: A Bond of Peace for the Sake of Love*, written by the Bishop of the Episcopal Diocese of Texas, the Right Rev. C. Andrew Doyle. The book ultimately addresses the issue of the blessing of same-sex marriages, as enacted by General Convention in 2012 and 2015. However, Bishop Doyle spends a good deal of time (as will we) considering more fundamental questions like the mission of the Church, the role of bishops, marks of the Anglican tradition, the interpretation of scripture and the nature of Christian marriage.

We plan to meet nine times to discuss a portion of the paper, which we'll have read in advance. Discussion questions for the next week's reading will also be distributed in advance, as they were for today's meeting. That we may be open to the influence of God's Word and the Holy Spirit, we will begin and end in a brief scripture reading and prayer. Following the opening prayer, we'll spend a little time responding to a Getting On Board question, in order to initiate our engagement with the topic and to help deepen our friendship. Each session provides a supplementary reading, which this group may elect to do or not do.

The intent of the study as a whole is not only to encounter some new ideas and insights, but also to take part in the "divine training that comes by faith" which St. Paul commended to Timothy. In this way we may grow together in love. Let's approach our training, and the Holy One who inspires it, with the reading and prayer printed on your handout.

II. Approach—5 minutes

Leader   Let the words of our mouths and the meditations of our hearts
People   be acceptable in your sight, O Lord, our strength and our
            redeemer.

                                                            – Psalm 19:14

Reader   A reading from the First Letter of Paul to Timothy.

I urge you, as I did when I was on my way to Macedonia, to remain in Ephesus so that you may instruct certain people not to teach any different doctrine, and not to occupy themselves with myths and endless genealogies that promote speculations rather than the divine training that is known by faith. But the aim of such instruction is love that comes from a pure heart, a good conscience, and sincere faith.

– I Timothy 1:3-5

Silence for reflection

Leader   Let us pray....

O God, you first taught the faithful by the light of your Holy Spirit. Grant that we may receive the divine training through the same Spirit, to grow in love and heartfulness, in conscience and in sincerity of faith. Through Christ our Lord. Amen.

III. Getting on Board Question—7 minutes

Tell the group your name, why you came to this study group and what you hope to gain from it.

IV. Discussion of Study Questions—25 minutes

The reading for today includes the preliminary portions of *Unity in Mission*. These are the remarks by Secretary James Baker and the Introduction by Bishop Doyle which explain how the paper came to be written. We've also assigned and will discuss Chapter Five: *Our Response* because the "Conversation Covenant" it describes can serve as a model for our own discussions.

Q1. What in the reading assigned for this first session strikes or impresses you, either positively or negatively?

A. Considering the opening material:

Q2. Review Charles Swindoll's definitions of union, uniformity, unanimity and unity.

"Union has an affiliation with others but no common bond that makes them one in heart. Uniformity has everyone looking and thinking alike. Unanimity is complete agreement across the board. Unity, however, refers to a oneness of heart, a similarity of purpose and an agreement on major points of doctrine."

What would be some examples of each of these four versions of commonality?

Union—the United States, stockholders in a corporation
Uniformity—a street gang, certain companies with a strong corporate culture, certain cliques
Unanimity—a unanimous vote or judicial opinion
Unity—many non-profit organizations, such as The Heifer Project, The Nature Conservancy

Which of these versions of commonality does your Church exhibit, if any? How about your congregation?

Q3. Why do you think the issue of same-sex relations is so divisive, as Secretary James Baker III and Bishop Doyle both assert?

Sexuality is so intimate for us and is tied to some of our deepest needs and fears. We all have some kind of personal issue with it.

Q4. Secretary Baker mentions in his statement "the Church's long history of allowing for decision-making at the local levels." Which Church do you think he is referring to?

He most likely means the Anglican Church, although he may mean the Church as a whole. Certainly some other denominations allow more local decision-making than we do; for example, the Congregational and Baptist Churches and the Churches of Christ. However, the Anglican Church certainly allows more local decision-making than certain others, like the Roman Catholic Church.

Q5. Bishop Doyle holds that at least parts of The Episcopal Church have "suffered, because of the belief that we should all agree on the matter of same-sex blessings, and that those who disagree should leave." Have you or your congregation suffered in this regard or do you know of anyone who has? Tell what has happened.

Responding to this question may have a wholesome effect for some participants. Walter Brueggemann, the Old Testament scholar, has said that healing may take place when pain can come to speech.

Q6. Bishop Doyle cites Romans 14:1 "quarreling over opinions" as poor stewardship of our time and energy. The longer passage is worth our reading. Here's Romans 14:1-7.

Welcome those who are weak in faith, but not for the purpose of quarrelling over opinions. Some believe in eating anything, while the weak eat only vegetables. Those who eat must not despise those who abstain, and those who abstain must not pass judgment on those who eat; for God has welcomed them. Who are you to pass judgment on servants of another? It is before their own lord that they stand or fall. And they will be upheld, for the Lord is able to make them stand.

Some judge one day to be better than another, while others judge all days to be alike. Let all be fully convinced in their own minds. Those who observe the day, observe it in honor of the Lord. Also those who eat, eat in honor of the Lord, since they give thanks to God; while those who abstain, abstain in honor of the Lord and give thanks to God.

We do not live to ourselves, and we do not die to ourselves.

How might these disputes concerning diet and the calendar apply to the issue of blessing same-sex unions, or do they?

These verses introduce the key concept of adiaphora, *which Bishop Doyle will explores. The ancient theological term* adiaphora *refers to "matters regarded as non-essential, issues about which one can disagree without dividing the Church."[1] Most strong traditionalists and strong progressives would claim that the blessing of same-sex relationships is not* adiaphora—*traditionalists saying the practice cannot be tolerated, progressives that it must be embraced. Bishop Doyle will point out that "within our Church there are a growing number of individuals who would indeed say that our uniformity on the sacrament of marriage is indeed* adiaphora."

St. Paul makes the point that, even in matters of "indifference," we make our choices

---

[1] *The Windsor Report* (2004) ¶ 87.

not simply to please ourselves.

Q7. Secretary Baker impressed the bishop by his insistence that being a leader entails taking stands that some people may not like. Would you agree? Have you ever exhibited this sort of leadership or seen it demonstrated in others?

Q8. What is Bishop Doyle's objective in writing *Unity in Mission*?

He writes: "I am seeking in this short text to answer the questions: How do people with differing views on sexuality and blessing of same-sex relationships stay together for the sake of the Gospel? How is it that we are able to remain one church?"

Q9. The Bishop confesses that the people of his diocese make him want to be a better bishop. This recalls the pivotal moment in the movie *As Good As It Gets* when Helen Hunt on a dinner date with the scurrilous Jack Nicholson insists that he give her a compliment. He fumbles, but says finally, "You make me want to be a better man."

More than one person has said, "Bishop Doyle makes me want to be a better priest." Who or what makes you want to be a better Christian?

B. Considering Chapter 8 *A Communal Response*:

Q11. Do you believe that trustful conversation can lead to "our common and communal transformation" or are such hopes in conversation misplaced?

The expectation that this conversation may lead us to communal transformation in the power of the Spirit underlies the reason for Christian formation and for encouraging such study groups as these. As Martin Buber said, "All real living is meeting."

Q12. How can "this moment of deep conflict and divide" possibly be a "sacred moment?"

Because the moment offers us the possibility of overcoming the divide and remaining steadfast in our commitments. Reconciliation is the sacred work which Christ Jesus gives us, potentially to "light a fire" and bear witness to the Church and to the world.

Q13. What ideas or phrases from chapter five would you like to adopt for this study group?

We suggest writing these on newsprint or a whiteboard.

Q14. What other agreements might the group make to strengthen your participation and experience here?

Participants might suggest confidentiality; a balance of sharing and listening; not giving unsolicited advice; arriving, starting and ending on time; doing the assigned readings. These should be added to the list on the newsprint and an agreement reached.

V. Optional Material—5 minutes

Because our text *Unity in Mission* is fundamentally about mission and because Bishop Doyle is fundamentally about mission, let's take a broader look at just what the Bishop understands our mission to be. The following reading is taken from his book *Unabashedly Episcopalian.*

The Heart of How the Episcopal Church Proclaims the Good News

Several themes are at the heart of this uniquely Episcopal proclamation of the good news, and we share these convictions globally with other Anglicans. They are captured in the bedrock of our Baptismal Covenant. They guide our living of the gospel message:

1. Our Episcopal faith is supported by our continued reflection on Scripture, the apostles' teachings, communal prayer, and life lived in connection with the sacraments.

2. Mission is the work of God, who was sent into the world and sends us into the world. When we enact the gospel, we make Jesus Christ incarnate in the world. Mission and outreach are about Jesus: first, last and always.

3. Mission and outreach are holistic. We seek to meet the needs of the whole person, spiritual and physical.

4. We proclaim in voice and in action the good news of the reign of God.

5. We teach, baptize and nurture believers.

6. We respond to human need by serving others.

7. We transform the unjust structures of society.

8. We seek sustainable and renewing initiatives that redeem not only humanity but the creation in which we live.

9. Our outreach and mission are always rooted in Scripture, tradition and reason.

10. We make a greater witness to the world around us when we join hands with one another beyond differences of theology, ideology, and identity, in order to meet the human needs around us.

11. We are changed by serving and walking with others. We are incomplete without the poor, voiceless, and oppressed by our side.

12. We are saved and given power to serve and act only by God's grace.

This is the unique story of our faith. It is the rock upon which my life rests. It is the particular story which gives meaning to the chaos of a world ruled by powers and principalities.
It is what we have been given by Jesus of Nazareth and what we have to offer the world.[2]

Discussion Questions

1. What do you understand to be the Church's mission?

2. Do any of Bishop Doyle's 12 points especially speak to you? Are there any you think should not be included? Are there any you would add?

3. You might wish to consider how these points arise out of the Baptismal Covenant in the *Book of Common Prayer* on pp. 304-305.

---

[2] Andrew Doyle, *Unabashedly Episcopalian* (Morehouse Publishing, 2012), pp. 87-88.

VI. Conclusion—5 minutes

Reader A reading from the Gospel according to John:

I ask not only on behalf of these, but also on behalf of those who will believe in me through their word, that they may all be one. As you, Father, are in me and I am in you, may they also be in us, so that the world may believe that you have sent me. The glory that you have given me I have given them, so that they may be one, as we are one, I in them and you in me, that they may be completely one, so that the world may know that you have sent me and have loved them even as you have loved me.

--John 17:20-23

Free intercessions and thanksgivings

The Lord's Prayer

Leader   Let us pray together:

All O Father, grant that our inner being may be strengthened through your Spirit and that Christ may dwell in our hearts through faith, as we are rooted and grounded in love. May we have the power to comprehend, with all the saints, what is the breadth and length and height and depth and know the love of Christ that surpasses all knowledge, so that we may be filled with all the fullness of God. To you who, working within us, are able to accomplish abundantly far more than all we can ask or imagine—to you be glory in the church and in Christ Jesus to all generations, forever and ever. Amen.

– adapted from Ephesians 3:15-20

After Session One:
The facilitator should type up the list of shared agreement and distribute copies at the next session.

Session Two
The Future We Create

I. Approach—5 minutes

Leader   Blessed are the peacemakers,
People   for they will be called children of God.

— *Matthew 5:9*

Reader   A reading from the Second Letter of Paul to the
             Corinthians…

So if anyone is in Christ, there is a new creation: everything old has passed away; see, everything has become new! All this is from God, who reconciled us to himself through Christ, and has given us the ministry of reconciliation….So we are ambassadors for Christ, since God is making his appeal through us; we entreat you on behalf of Christ, be reconciled to God.

— *2 Corinthians 5:17-18, 20*

Silence for reflection

Leader   Let us pray…

O God unto whom all hearts lie open
unto whom desire is eloquent
and from whom no secret thing is hidden;
purify the thoughts of our hearts
by the outpouring of your Spirit
that we may love you with a perfect love
and praise you as you deserve. Amen.

— *adapted from the opening prayer of* The Cloud of Unknowing

II. Getting on Board Question—7 minutes

What has been one of the hardest changes for you to undergo in your life? How have you managed to come through it?

III. Introduction—2 minutes

The facilitator should begin by distributing copies of the guidelines that the group arrived at during the last session. Participants should have the opportunity to ask questions, to offer changes and, finally, to commit to the guidelines.

Bishop Doyle, summarizes the decline in membership in the Episcopal Church since 1970 and considers its possible causes. He calls on sociological findings regarding change, the dynamics of conflict, and the culture wars. Finally, he quickly surveys the history of the Episcopal bishops of the Diocese of Texas, which probably parallels many other Episcopal dioceses. His purpose is to see how the bishops' approach to the conflicts of their day may inform church leaders today.

The optional supplementary material consists of portions of the new rite of blessing same-sex relationships, officially entitled "The Witnessing and Blessing of a Lifelong Covenant." This is the only opportunity in this course to engage the rite directly. (The Episcopal Church has published a document *Liturgical Resources 1: I Will Bless You, and You Will Be a Blessing: Resources for Blessing Same-Sex Relationships*, which includes the rite in full and a study course for congregations. If you are using this after Advent 2015 you will want to download from the General Convention Office or the Episcopal Church the latest liturgical materials available following the 2015 General Convention.)

IV. Discussion of Study Questions—25 minutes

Q1. What in this introductory chapter strikes or impresses you, either positively or negatively?

Q2. Bishop Doyle cites a lot of statistics regarding the decline in the number of members in the Episcopal Church since 1970. To what does he attribute this decline? Do you agree? Do you see the numerical decline as a problem?

He attributes the slide to our conflicts concerning sexuality. The quotation from Russell Levenson mentions other conflicts, such as women's ordination, prayer book revision, and civil rights. But Levenson also adds that the huge loss between 1970 and 1975 took place before the fiercest conflict over women and the prayer book.

One could point to broader cultural trends at the time that led to declining membership in mainline Protestant churches generally. This shift is often associated with a loss of trust in traditional institutions and is typically connected with such developments as the Vietnam War and the Watergate scandal.

Of course the numerical decline of the Episcopal Church is a problem for us.

Q3. What action does the Bishop recommend for reversing the decline? Do you agree?

He recommends that Episcopalians maintain their unity and friendship despite their disagreements. He also recommends planting new churches, proactive newcomer ministry and taking the Gospel to those outside our churches.

Q4. How might Philip Wylie's two principles:
  1) human nature does not change, and
  2) fashion and trends change offer insight toward resolving our disputes over sexuality?

Wylie's principles underscore the importance of process over content. Given human nature, disagreements and conflicts are inevitable. The task is as much to address the underlying dynamics of control, inclusion and affection as to address the current trend.

Q5. Consider the graph in chapter one. What does the vertical axis running to from 0 to 12 measure?

The intensity of conflict.

Have you ever experienced or witnessed people moving into "incapacity" as their conflict mounts?

Q6. What evidence do you see that we do or do not live in a "culture of indictment" in the United States at this time? A related question: What issues have stoked the culture wars and is the fight still continuing?

The term "culture wars" came into currency with the publication in 1991 of the book Culture Wars: A Struggle to Define America *by James Davison Hunter. This author believes that America, since the 1960s, has become polarized between the "orthodox" and "progressive" views regarding abortion, homosexuality, education, laws, censorship and the arts.*

Q7. What common theme does Bishop Doyle seem to find running through the history of the Episcopal bishops of Texas?

The importance of mission and overcoming our disagreements and divisions.

Q8. As you look back on the history of your congregation (or your diocese, or both) what common theme stands out for you?

Q9. What terms or ideas presented by the Bishop would you like to know more about?

Facilitator might suggest the individual follow up and bring the findings to the next class, something most people can easily do with the Internet.

V. Optional Supplementary Material—5 minutes

Before going any further in this course, we should move out of abstractions and look at the actual rites of same-sex marriage that the General Convention adopted in 2015 and that lies at the heart of the controversy. (For this exercise you will need a *Book of Common Prayer* and a copy of the *Liturgy Supplemental Materials: Appendices of the Report of the Standing Commission on Liturgy and Music* found on the General Convention website.)

Discussion Questions

1. What similarities and what differences do you notice between the two rites?

The structure and wording are very similar. However, the new rite avoids any sex-specific language, whereas the traditional rite is very sex-specific.

2. Does "The Witnessing and Blessing of a Lifelong Covenant" use any of the terminology of Holy Matrimony or indicate that an actual marriage is taking place? Look at the same-sex marriage rites, what words are used here?

In fact, the new rite does not mention the words "marriage" or "matrimony." You might consider why this is the case. Most people will have an opinion on whether this is a good thing or a bad one. What about the most recent approved liturgies in 2015? What draws your attention here?

3. Does any part of the new rite indicate that the participants are two men or two women?

The rite chooses not to draw attention to the fact that the participants are the same sex. Again people will have varying opinions on whether this is best.

VI. Conclusion—5 minutes

Reader A reading from the Letter of James.

Every generous act of giving, with every perfect gift, is from above, coming down from the Father of lights, with whom there is no variation or shadow due to change. In fulfillment of his own purpose he gave us birth by the word of truth, so that we would become a kind of first fruits of his creatures. …Therefore welcome with meekness the implanted word which has power to save your souls. But be doers of the word, and not merely hearers.

– James 1:17-18, 21b-22

Free intercessions and thanksgivings

The Lord's Prayer

Leader Let us pray together:

All   Thou, O Father
Thou, O Son
Thou, O Spirit
  only one.
Amend our minds, O Father.
  Our bodies tend, O Son.
  Align our spirits, Spirit.
      Make us one.[3] *– Andrew Parker*

---

[3] This prayer is rooted in the idea developed by St. Augustine of Hippo that every human being is tripartite, reflecting the image of the Trinity. The prayer may be modified for individual use by changing the plural forms to the singular,

Session Three
The Responsibility of the Bishop as Leader

I. Approach—5 minutes

Leader   Send out your light and your truth that they may lead me
People   and bring me to your holy hill and to your dwelling.
                                                        – *Psalm 43:3*

Reader   A reading from the Letter of Paul to Titus

For a bishop, as God's steward, must be blameless; he must not be arrogant or quick-tempered or addicted to wine or violent or greedy for gain; but he must be hospitable, a lover of goodness, prudent, upright, devout, and self-controlled. He must have a firm grasp of the word that is trustworthy in accordance with the teaching, so that he may be able to both preach with sound doctrine and to refute those who contradict it.
                                                        – *Titus 1:7-9*

Silence for reflection

Leader   Let us pray….

To you, O Father, all hearts are open; fill, we pray, the hearts of all your servants whom you have chosen to be bishops in your Church, with such love of you and of all the people, that they may feed and tend the flock of Christ, serving before you day and night in the ministry of reconciliation, declaring pardon in your Name, offering the holy gifts, and wisely overseeing the life and work of the Church. May we, with them, present before you the acceptable offering of a pure, and gentle, and holy life; through Jesus Christ, our Lord. *Amen.*
                                            – *adapted from the BCP p.521*

II. Getting on Board Question—8 minutes

What has been your personal experience of bishops? More specifically, have you had a favorite bishop? What did you appreciate about him or her?

---

as in "Amend my mind, O Father…"

III. Introduction—2 minutes

In this first chapter proper, Bishop Doyle explores and articulates the Anglican understanding of the role of bishop. He does so in order to make clear right up front his theological and historical reasons for writing and for taking on such a controversial, complex topic. The chapter introduces a number of themes that will inform the paper as a whole and will lead toward the "Plan" found in chapter six. Examples are the missionary church, reconciliation, distinguishing essentials from the nonessentials, the issue of divorce, enculturation and catholicity.

Before going further, we should consider the meaning of the term *catholic*, a word Bishop Doyle favors but which is used so variously. We can distinguish at least three senses, moving from broad to narrower meanings:

(1) *Catholic* is derived from the Greek word *katholikos*, which means "whole," "general" or "universal." This use describes "the universal Church as distinct from local Christian communities. It is applied thus to the faith of the whole Church."[4]

(2) *Catholic* may designate "the Church before the great schism between East and West, or any Church standing in historical continuity with it,"[5] such as the Roman Catholic, Eastern Orthodox and Anglican Churches. These branches acknowledge the authority of the church councils prior to the great schism and preserve the apostolic succession of bishops and many components of the ancient liturgy.

(3) "Since the Reformation, the Roman Catholics have come to use the term of themselves exclusively."[6]

Bishop Doyle tends to use *catholic* in the second sense.

IV. Discussion of Study Questions—25 minutes

[4] *The Oxford Dictionary of the Christian Church* (Oxford University Press, 1990), p. 254.

[5] *The New Shorter Oxford English Dictionary* (Clarendon Press, Oxford, 1993), p. 354.

[6] *The Oxford Dictionary of the Christian Church* (Oxford University Press, 1990), p. 254.

Q1. What in this chapter strikes or impresses you, either positively or negatively?

Q2. In the chapter's opening paragraph, Bishop Doyle states that he is a bishop of the Diocese of Texas, a bishop in the Episcopal Church and a bishop within the Anglican Communion, in that order. He adds: "In our common life we may think that we reverse this hierarchy, but in reality I am rooted in my place of ministry."

Why do you think Bishop Doyle chooses to rank the hierarchy from local to global? Would you agree?

Consider the power of the particular, the specific and the local. Many writers will tell you that "you cannot write from anywhere unless you write from somewhere" or, as Billy Collins puts it, "You cannot start in Oz. You have to start in Kansas." Similarly, one of the pioneers of psychotherapy, Carl Rogers, said "that which is most personal is most universal."

In the twelfth chapter of the book of Genesis, the Lord turned from saving humanity in general to calling and saving a specific people, the Jews. The Son of God was incarnated as a particular human being at a particular time and place.

Q3. "We cannot use dogma, which we believe is essential, to bludgeon our fellow Christians or those who seek a living Christ. We must be faithful to the Gospel, but we cannot condemn the mission field we wish to convert or condemn one another."

What is dogma, actually? Why is it essential? Has someone ever "bludgeoned" you with dogma?

The word dogma comes from a Greek word meaning "to seem good" or "an opinion." Thus a dogma is a belief or doctrine that an authoritative council has considered and declared "good." For example, the doctrines of the Trinity and the Incarnation were defined by the first four general councils of the Church and given the status of dogma, meaning they are definitive and normative for the Church.

Dogma gives shape to our faith and provides a given place on which we may stand. Dogma helps to distinguish the essential from the nonessential.

Q4. An Inter-Anglican Theological Commission describes *koinonia* as "the intimate communion of God" and asserts that "the challenge for bishops is how to harness conflicts so that through this process a deeper *koinonia* in the Gospel emerges."

Have you had any experiences of *koinonia?*

Has your *koinonia* with another person, or a group of people, ever deepened as a result of working through a conflict?

Koinonia is sometimes translated as "fellowship" and describes the communion we have with one another through God.

Frequently, couples in a marriage or a romantic relationship find that their relationship is deepened by working through a conflict.

Q5. In the paper the bishop writes, "Diversity is not a core value of our faith—catholicity is."

What do you see as the difference between the concepts of "diversity" and "catholicity"?

Catholicity presupposes an underlying unity and common ground...referenced by the TSEO as the "fullness of the one faith." (p.27) The local expression differs, but the substance is held in common. (One could draw an analogy with the Trinity, in which the Father, Son and Holy Spirit all "express" the same substance.)

Q6. In addition to catholicity, what other values are also "core" for Bishop Doyle? How would you agree or disagree?

Some of the prominent core values in this chapter are unity, mission, reconciliation, proclamation and evangelism, "every person's deeply cherished experience of God and nearness to God," the "theological legacy of scripture, tradition and reason" and the history and heritage of the Diocese of Texas.

Q7. A related question: What various vocations (or roles) does Bishop Doyle wish to live out?

He touches on these vocations throughout the chapter and they are conveniently summarized with these words: "This is my vocation as bishop—to be: chief liturgist, an evangelist, an apostolic teacher and binder of our faith, a partner with clergy and laity alike, a mediator of God's grace, an encourager of reconciliation, catholic and a colleague with my brother and sister bishops."

Q8. What are your vocations in life? How are your vocations shaped by your identity as a Christian? Have you ever found yourself doing your work "without these vocations in the forefront" of your mind?

Q9. Bishop Doyle includes an extended quote from an Inter-Anglican theological document on the subject of enculturation.
What is meant by enculturation? How does this concept bear upon the "challenge posed by division" and the blessing of same-sex relationships?

To use Bishop Doyle's words, enculturation "translates locally what is received from abroad." All Anglicans have "received" the catholic faith and, with it, the Christian understanding of marriage. How this is "translated" will vary from culture to culture, nation to nation, possibly even from congregation to congregation.

Q10. Have you ever experienced "the stumbling blocks that diversity brings" either in the church or another setting? How was it resolved, if at all?

Q11. Do you agree as Bishop Doyle says, that "we hide from our catholicity with words like *conservatives* or *traditionalists* and *liberals* or *progressives?*"

Why do we adopt these words?

Such words help us define our identity.

Q12. To what negative experiences of Church might Bishop Doyle be responding in this chapter?

People using dogma like a bludgeon. Bishops (or other Episcopalians) depreciating their bonds with each other.

Q13. How does the Bishop's "stand" described in the final paragraph of the chapter strike you?

Participants might choose words such as "heroic," "pompous," "obedient," "authentic," "conscientious" or "courageous." The facilitator doesn't need to argue for or against any of these.

Why does he feel the necessity to take a stand?

He feels this is his responsibility as Bishop Diocesan. Secretary James Baker told him: "We need you to be our bishop. No, not everyone will like what you are proposing, but this is what it means to be a leader." The Secretary also advised him: "Bishop, you have to decide where you are on this issue. Then people can decide where they are, in relation to you."

Q14. What major point(s) do you believe Bishop Doyle is trying to get across in this first chapter?

Two of these major points:
1. Bishop Doyle has undertaken this Paper and Plan in the midst of our crisis because of his understanding of his role as leader and bishop of the diocese.
2. As bishop, his vocation is to be: "chief liturgist, an evangelist, an apostolic teacher and binder of our faith, a partner with clergy and laity alike, a mediator of God's grace, an encourager of reconciliation, catholic and a colleague with my brother and sister bishops."

Q15. What terms or ideas presented by the Bishop would you like to know more about?

Facilitator might again suggest the individual follow-up and bring the findings to the next class.

V. Optional Supplementary Material: Enculturation—5 minutes

Evangelism and the Wholeness of Mission by the Rt. Revd. Michael

Nazir-Ali, Bishop of Rochester, England[7]

Kerygma means the core belief, the bare bones of Christian faith, and of course *kerygma* is related to proclamation. It is in the proclamation, in the preaching, that you discover what the core is. You don't sit down somewhere and write a tome of systematic theology to discover what the bare bones of the Christian faith are. You discover that in the preaching itself. That is pretty basic. The difficulty of course is that evangelists are preaching in different contexts. They are not preaching in a monocultural situation. Certainly in the United Kingdom now, even in a parish the situation is not monocultural. People of different cultures, different world views, different value systems are living cheek by jowl. So how is the preaching to be done and the bare bones of the faith to be discerned? The point is that it is done in context.

In the New Testament, already we find that when the preaching is given to the Jewish people, as in the great kerygmatic speeches in the Acts of the Apostles, the whole of salvation history is rehearsed; how God has been working among those people and now how he is bringing them back to a fulfilment of the story of Jesus. But when the Gospel has to be preached to those who have no such Jewish background, then the evangelists take a different line. Can you think of any examples in the New Testament of where that happens?...You mention Athens. Paul is left alone in Athens, but as a good Jew his spirit rebels against the idolatry that he sees all around. Yet, when he comes to his speech in the Areopagus he begins with the native religious sense of the Athenians and he tries to connect with them, not only with the reference to the unknown God but the quotations that he uses from the Greek poems. "In him we live and move and have our being." That was not said by a Jew. It is not in the Old Testament. So this is what St. Paul means I suppose when he says to the Jew I became a Jew, to the Gentile I became a Gentile (I Corinthians 9). You see it is not just an external thing that you proclaim the Gospel to people in one way but you believe it in another way yourself. That is not authentic enculturation or contextualization. You know, when missionaries came to

---

[7] A selection from a much longer address to the Inter-Anglican Provincial Mission and Evangelism Co-ordinators Consultation in Nairobi, Kenya in May 2002, lightly edited for this curriculum. The original address may be found in full here:
www.anglicancommunion.org/ministry/mission/resources/papers/paper2.cfm

Pakistan, they were told they mustn't place the Bible on the floor, because that is a cultural value. But as soon as they returned home, they put the Bible back on the floor—I mean they have not learned anything! So proclamation necessarily leads us to ask the question to whom is the Gospel being proclaimed....

Now when we try to relate the Gospel to culture....we still have to ask what are the limits to enculturation. The Pope in an Encyclical written some years ago said that there were two: The nature of the Gospel itself is a limit. You can't compromise that. And the fellowship between believers is another limit, so that I should not do anything in my preaching and living the gospel that compromises you. This is for the Anglican tradition a first order question—that we must recognise and respect the gospel in one another and make sure that we are not a stumbling block for our brother or sister in another context.

I used to feel this when working on the Indian border. I was Bishop of Raiwind, almost on the Indian border, and at that time we could cross over into India to spend the day. As soon as you crossed the border, you could see the difference, but not only do you see the difference in life generally, but also in how people worship, how they handle the scriptures. In Pakistan, people are, of necessity influenced by their Islamic environment, they want to be Christians in an Islamic environment, worship is therefore simple, Bible-centred, preaching orientated and so forth. You cross over into India and there is incense and candles and flowers and colour and all sorts of things. And I used to ask myself the question: When would Christians in Pakistan cease to see the faith in their brothers and sisters in India, because the expression of the faith has become so different? That must be a concern with us all the time.

Discussion Questions
1. What is your understanding of enculturation?

2. How might the insistence of the Anglican reformers that public worship be "in a tongue understanded of the people"[8] be an example of enculturation?

3. What are the limits to enculturation, according to the address?

---

[8] Article XXIV of *The Articles of Religion, BCP* p. 872.

(1) The nature of the gospel and (2) the fellowship between the believers.

4. How do these limits apply to our controversy regarding the blessing of same-sex relationships?

First, we must discern whether blessing these relationships is universally excluded by the "kerygma," the core faith. If not, then we must consider how the implementation of the blessing may best be done without offending the consciences of others or impairing our fellowship.

VI. Conclusion—5 minutes

Reader A reading from the Second Letter of Paul to the Corinthians.

You are a letter of Christ, prepared by us, written not with ink but with the Spirit of the living God, not on tablets of stone but on tablets of human hearts. Such is the confidence that we have through Christ toward God. Not that we are competent of ourselves to claim anything as coming from us; our competence is from God, who has made us competent to be ministers of a new covenant, not of letter but of spirit; for the letter kills, but the Spirit gives life.

– 2 Corinthians 3:3-6

Free intercessions and thanksgivings

The Lord's Prayer

Leader   Let us pray together:

All O God of truth and peace, you raise up your servants in days of bitter controversy to defend with sound reasoning and great charity the catholic and reformed religion: Grant that we may maintain that middle way, not as a compromise for the sake of peace, but as a comprehension for the sake of truth; through Jesus Christ our Lord, who lives and reigns with you and the Holy Spirit, one God, for ever and ever. Amen.

– adapted from the Collect for Richard Hooker, LFF p. 427

Session Four
Unity: Effective Instrument of Mission, Part I

I. Approach—5 minutes

Leader	Thy word is a lamp unto my feet;
People	And a light unto my path.

— Psalms 119:105

Reader   A reading from the Letter of Paul to the Ephesians:

So then you are no longer strangers and aliens, but you are citizens with the saints and also members of the household of God, built upon the foundation of the apostles and prophets, with Christ Jesus himself as the cornerstone. In him the whole structure is joined together and grows into a holy temple in the Lord; in whom you also are built together spiritually into a dwelling-place for God.

— Ephesians 2:19-22

Silence for reflection

Leader
Almighty God, you have built your Church upon the foundation of the apostles and prophets, Jesus Christ himself being the chief cornerstone: Grant us so to be joined together in unity of spirit by their teaching, that we may be made a holy temple acceptable to you; through Jesus Christ our Lord, who lives and reigns with you and the Holy Spirit, one God, for ever and ever. *Amen.*

— BCP 230, Collect for Proper 8

II. Getting on Board Question—8 minutes

Bishop Doyle writes, "As a congregation or as a diocese it is our responsibility to engage the scripture." How have you taken responsibility for engaging scripture in your own life?

III. Introduction—2 minutes

Bishop Doyle turns his attention to the question, "What unites us as Episcopalians and as Anglicans if not our stance on human sexuality?" Doyle identifies four "marks" that unify us as Episcopalians and Anglicans.

These marks are the basis of our unity and are (1) scripture, (2) worship, (3) our particular orders of communion and our (4) mission. In the first half of chapter two, Bishop Doyle lays the groundwork for the conversation and then turns his attention to the first mark of our unity, which is scripture.

Episcopalians, Doyle argues, are united by the studying of the scriptures. It is God's living and active word and the primary basis for "our churches' decision-making." As Anglicans we read the scriptures not just privately but in the *context* of community. Context matters greatly for how Episcopalians interpret scripture. The study of the scripture is "at the center of our unity." We hold it to be "authoritative."

However, the *authority* of scripture is defined uniquely by Anglicans as "the authority of the triune God, exercised through scripture" (*The Windsor Report*). We define authority in this way for two reasons. First, scripture itself states that all authority belongs to Him (Matthew 28:18). Jesus alone is "God's ultimate and personal self-expression" (TWR). Second, as Doyle states, "It is this understanding that keeps Anglicans and Episcopalians from becoming narrow in their reading of the text." In other words, Episcopalians are hesitant to take a text and apply it universally. Rather, we see an Anglican reading of scripture as a dynamic, revelatory practice, which happens as we read the Bible both privately and in community.

The study of scripture is the responsibility of the Episcopalian. We are called to "read, mark and inwardly digest" the scriptures. We have made a vow before God and the church to continue in the apostles' teaching (*Baptismal Covenant*). Such is why for the Episcopalians scripture is an "essential guidepost" and a mark of our unity.

IV. Discussion of Study Questions—25 minutes

Q1. What in this chapter strikes or impresses you, either positively or negatively?

Q2. Bishop Doyle references our "sinful want to fight rather than to engage in mission." Do you believe fighting is often "easier" than in engaging in the difficult work of mission? Why or why not?

Fighting is often the way we try and protect our fragile ego. We want to be "right" and it makes us feel "safe." Mission, on the other hand, is a call to take up our cross daily and to lose our life, serving others, for the sake of the Gospel. It is inherently "unsafe."

Q3. Bishop Doyle quotes St. Paul in arguing that we are called to be "in full accord and one mind." How can we be of "one mind" and still disagree on important theological issues?

The "mind" Paul is referencing in Philippians 2 is the "mind of Christ," expressed most fully in a willingness to go to the cross for the other. Fighting and bickering is utterly opposed to this "mind." Two people may disagree on the presenting issue of the day, but if they have Jesus' mind they can unite for the sake of mission.

Q4. Bishop Doyle suggests that the most appropriate way to be in relationship with others is to "empty ourselves in order to be filled with grace?" What does this look like in practice? Can you offer any example?

I am reminded of John the Baptist's words with respect to Jesus: "He must increase, I must decrease" (John 3:30). Jesus' parable of the great banquet also comes to mind. The one who takes the lowest place is told, "Friend, come up higher!" (Luke 14:10)

Q5. We have a collect that calls us to "read, mark and inwardly digest the scriptures." What does this look like in practice? How do you live this out in your own life?

Here would be a good place to be reminded of Peterson's quote, i.e., that "reading scripture constitutes an act of crisis" as it "brings us into a world that is totally at odds" with the world we encounter. We cannot live in this world and not "inwardly digest" its beliefs, values and assumptions. When we read scripture we "take in" the beliefs, values and assumptions of a "new world" Jesus called the Kingdom of God. Perhaps the goal of scripture is for Jesus' world to become more real to us than the one we're sold by the media, and for that to change how we live in our world as a result.

Q6. What does the term "authority of scripture" mean for an Anglican? Why can this term be misleading?

This is a shorthand term for "God's authority exercised through scripture." All authority belongs to God and the Bible is the primary way God exercises that authority. As a result it must be read in its context, and always in community. Even though the Bible is without error, it is only without error with respect to the purposes God has in mind for it. In other words, the Bible, as a means of exercising God's authority is infallible, but when we use it for our purposes we most certainly are fallible.

V. Optional Supplementary Material: Biblical Authority

Excerpt from "How Can the Bible be Authoritative?"
Rt. Rev. N.T. Wright
To read full article:
http://ntwrightpage.com/Wright_Bible_Authoritative.htm
The Bible and Biblical Authority

[I]f we are to get to the authority of scripture, how does God exercise that authority? Again and again, in the biblical story itself we see that he does so through human agents anointed and equipped by the Holy Spirit. And this is itself an expression of his love, because he does not will, simply to come into the world in a blinding flash of light and obliterate all opposition. He wants to reveal himself meaningfully within the space/time universe not just passing it by tangentially; to reveal himself in judgment and in mercy in a way which will save people. So, we get the prophets. We get obedient writers in the Old Testament, not only prophets but those who wrote the psalms and so on. As the climax of the story we get Jesus himself as the great prophet, but how much more than a prophet. And, we then get Jesus' people as the anointed ones. And within that sequence there is a very significant passage, namely 1 Kings 22. Micaiah, the son of Imlah (one of the great prophets who didn't leave any writing behind him but who certainly knew what his business was), stands up against the wicked king, Ahab. The false prophets of Israel at the time were saying to Ahab, 'Go up against Ramoth-gilead and fight and you will triumph. Yahweh will give it into your hand'. This is especially interesting, because the false prophets appear to have everything going for them. They are quoting Deuteronomy 33—one of them makes horns and puts them on his head and says, "with these you will crush the enemy until they are overthrown." They had scripture on their side, so it seemed. They had tradition on their side; after all, Yahweh was the God of Battles and he would fight for Israel. They had reason on their side; Israel and Judah together can beat these northern enemies quite easily. But they didn't have God on their side. Micaiah had stood in the council of the Lord and in that private, strange, secret meeting he had learned that even the apparent scriptural authority which these prophets had, and the apparent tradition and reason, wasn't good enough; God wanted to judge Ahab and so save Israel. And so God delegated his authority to the prophet Micaiah who, inspired by the Spirit, stood humbly in the council of God and then stood boldly in the councils of men. He put his life and liberty on the line, like Daniel and so many others. That is how God brought his authority to bear on Israel: not by revealing to them a set of timeless truths, but by delegating his authority to obedient men through whose words he brought judgment and salvation to Israel and the world.

And how much more must we say of Jesus. Jesus the great prophet; Jesus who rules from the cross in judgment and love; Jesus who says: all authority is given to me, so you go and get on with the job. I hope the irony of that has not escaped you. So too in Acts 1, we find: God has all authority . . . so that you will receive power. Again, the irony. How can we resolve that irony? By holding firmly to what the New Testament gives us, which is the strong theology of the authoritative Holy Spirit. Jesus' people are to be the anointed ones through whom God still works authoritatively. And then, in order that the church may be the church—may be the people of God for the world—God, by that same Holy Spirit, equips men in the first generation to write the new covenant documentation. This is to be the new covenant documentation that gives the foundation charter and the characteristic direction and identity to the people of God, who are to be the people of God for the world. It is common to say in some scholarly circles that the evangelists, for instance, didn't know they were writing scripture. One of the gains of modern scholarship is that we now see that to be a mistake. Redaction criticism has shown that Matthew, Mark, Luke and John were writing what they were writing in order that it might be the foundation documentation for the church of their day and might bear God's authority in doing so. And a book which carries God's authority to be the foundation of the church for the world is what I mean by scripture. I think they knew what they were doing.

Thus it is that through the spoken and written authority of anointed human beings God brings his authority to bear on his people and his world. Thus far, we have looked at what the Bible says about how God exercises his judging and saving authority. And it includes (the point with which in fact we began) the delegation of his authority, in some sense, to certain writings. But this leads us to more questions.

When we turn the question round, however, and ask it the other way about, we discover just what a rich concept of authority we are going to need if we are to do justice to this book. The writings written by these people, thus led by the Spirit, are not for the most part, as we saw, the sort of things we would think of as "authoritative." They are mostly narrative; and we have already run up against the problem how can a story, a narrative, be authoritative? Somehow, the authority that God has invested in this book is an authority that is wielded and exercised through the people of God telling and retelling their story as the story of the world, telling the covenant story as the true story of creation. Somehow, this authority is also wielded through his people singing psalms. Somehow, it is wielded (it seems) in particular through God's people telling the story of Jesus.

Discussion Questions:

Is the Bible the only way God exercises His authority? How else might God exercise His authority, or "speak," to us? Would the Bible have any authority if there were no one to read it? Why or why not?

VI. Conclusion—5 minutes

Reader A reading from the Second Letter of Paul to Timothy.

But as for you, continue in what you have learned and firmly believed, knowing from whom you learned it, and how from childhood you have known the sacred writings that are able to instruct you for salvation through faith in Christ Jesus. All scripture is inspired by God and is useful for teaching, for reproof, for correction, and for training in righteousness, so that everyone who belongs to God may be proficient, equipped for every good work.

– 2 Timothy 3:14-17

Free intercessions and thanksgivings

The Lord's Prayer

Leader

Blessed Lord, who caused all holy Scriptures to be written for our learning: Grant us so to hear them, read, mark, learn, and inwardly digest them, that we may embrace and ever hold fast the blessed hope of everlasting life, which you have given us in our Savior Jesus Christ; who lives and reigns with you and the Holy Spirit, one God, for ever and ever. *Amen.*

– BCP 236, Collect for Proper 28

Session Five
Unity: Effective Instrument of Mission, Part 2

I. Approach—5 minutes

Leader   The Lord is in his holy temple;
People   let all the earth keep silence before him.

— Habakkuk 2:20

Reader   A reading from the Gospel according to Matthew

Now the eleven disciples went to Galilee, to the mountain to which Jesus had directed them. When they saw him, they worshipped him; but some doubted. And Jesus came and said to them, "All authority in heaven and on earth has been given to me. Go therefore and make disciples of all nations, baptizing them in the name of the Father and of the Son and of the Holy Spirit, and teaching them to obey everything that I have commanded you. And remember, I am with you always, to the end of the age."

— Matthew 28:16-20

Silence for reflection

Leader

O God, you have made of one blood all the peoples of the earth, and sent your blessed Son to preach peace to those who are far off and to those who are near: Grant that people everywhere may seek after you and find you; bring the nations into your fold; pour out your Spirit upon all flesh; and hasten the coming of your kingdom; through Jesus Christ our Lord. *Amen.*

— BCP 100, a Collect for Mission

II. Getting on Board Question—8 minutes

Have you experienced worship in more than one Episcopal Church? In what ways did the worship experiences differ? In what ways were they similar?

III. Introduction—2 minutes

Bishop Doyle turns his attention to the question, "What unites us as Episcopalians and as Anglicans if not our stance on human sexuality?" Doyle identifies four "marks" that unify us as Episcopalians and Anglicans. These marks are the basis of our unity and are (1) scripture, (2) worship, (3) our particular orders of communion and our (4) mission. In the second half of chapter two, Bishop Doyle turns his attention to marks 2-4: worship, how the Episcopal Church is uniquely ordered for communion and mission.

Doyle explains that worship is the second mark of our unity as Anglicans. He quotes Augustine to highlight our universal human need to praise God. It is primarily in the context of Episcopal worship, as we act on that instinct, that God challenges "us towards greater unity." In worship we receive our common identity and are reminded that we belong to God.

The third aspect of our unity as Episcopalians is found in the particular way we are ordered for communion. Particular emphasis is given to the role of bishops, whose primary function is to symbolize and safeguard the unity of the Church. "Those with ordered lives," Doyle says, "are called to support the baptized in their own ministries." As bishops engage one another formally and informally geographical divides are bridged.

"The fourth way we share a common journey with Episcopalians and Anglicans is through a common mission." Our "chief" work is to proclaim the Gospel of Salvation in word and deed. Doyle emphasizes the Anglican spirit of doing mission with context in mind. This is important to remember because ours is a context where we "differ on the presenting issues of the day" (i.e., human sexuality). Doyle asks us to acknowledge that at times our mission had been driven by abuse, self-interest and domination. His hope is that our motives in today's context will be different. He reminds us that our primary mission is to serve the weak and the poor.

It is these four marks of unity that make us distinct from the world around us and challenge us "to be about bringing into reality the Kingdom of God today." After discussing these four marks at length, Doyle gives special attention to the two Gospel Sacraments of Baptism and Eucharist, and how they differ from the other five sacraments with a little "s." His hope is to put marriage in its proper context, thereby putting the debate on human sexuality in its proper context.

Doyle closes this chapter by being clear about the hierarchy of elements that unify us. Doyle places "the creeds, historic councils, the three-fold order of ministry, and prayer book worship as primary and of the utmost concern to all in the communion. Entwined and linked to every one of these elements are the two Sacraments of the Anglican Church: Baptism and Eucharist."

Doyle says that only when this hierarchy is respected can we work for interdependence, rather than seeking a faithless form of independence. Doyle closes the chapter by reminding the reader, "I will work to preserve and hand on this faith as I have received it."

IV. Discussion of Study Questions—25 minutes

Q1. What in this chapter strikes or impresses you, either positively or negatively?

Q2. Bishop Doyle quotes Augustine's famous line, "our hearts are restless until they find their rest in [God]." Does this quote ring true in your own life? Where else are we tempted to find "rest" apart from God?

The leader might consider being vulnerable by disclosing his/her own restlessness and the many places he/she is tempted to find "rest" (security, well-being, significance) apart from God. Examples may include money, power, prestige, respect, their spouse/children, or reputation. We are reminded of Doyle's words that "our worship tells us who we are" and "whose we are." Idolatry is our human tendency to "find rest" or an identity in something other than God. Many people in the church seek "rest" and security in doctrinal correctness on the issue of human sexuality. We are reminded that Jesus' call to "repent" is a life-giving call to turn from our idols and find rest, yet again, in God alone.

Q3. Doyle says that the particular way we are ordered—bishops, priests, deacons and the laity—are a mark of unity in the Episcopal Church. How do you understand the role of ordained clergy? In what way is their vocation similar to that of the laity, and how is it different?

It will be helpful to recall Doyle's words that "those with ordered lives…are called to support the baptized in their own ministries." It is also good to be reminded that lay persons are listed first among the ministers of the church in our catechism, and that lay and ordained alike share a common vocation to "represent Christ and his Church." (BCP, 855)

Q4. "One of the unique hallmarks of our work as a church in mission is that we believe we do our mission in context." In what ways might the cultural context change the way the church engages in mission? In what ways is the church's mission the same across all cultural contexts?

The consistent mission of the church is to form disciples of Jesus Christ and to teach them to obey everything that Jesus commands (Matthew 28:16-20). What makes this difficult is that a disciple's job is to know Jesus' heart, so that he/she might do, through the power of the Spirit, what Jesus would do in any given context. Thus we see that the same action might be right in one context and wrong in another. Thus Paul can say in 1 Corinthians 8 that it is perfectly acceptable to eat meat offered to idols in one context, but against the Lord's will in another (i.e., if it causes a believer to "stumble"). Therefore, our common mission is to know and obey Jesus Christ no matter what the context. But because we are an "incarnational people," the obedient thing in one context might displease the Lord in another context. Such is why the Spirit's work is to "renew our mind" so that we might know the Lord's will in all circumstances. (Romans 12:2) Faithfulness, therefore, doesn't just require prayer, but good and hard "thinking" as well.

Q5. "We promise to work for justice, peace, and the dignity of every human being." In your own life, how would you rate your faithfulness at living into this baptismal promise? In what areas of your life might you do better, and what stops you from succeeding 100% of the time?

Hopefully no one gives themselves a grade of 100% faithfulness. It might be helpful for the leader to ask them how they are doing with members of their own family. It seems that the people that trigger our defensiveness routines most frequently are the ones we love the most. Thus, it is good to be reminded, in a chapter about what unites us, that what doesn't unite us is our own goodness or faithfulness. We all "miss the mark." The reasons for this are numerous. We are lazy and overwhelmed, and we have an instinctual drive to first and foremost protect our own sense of peace and dignity. Far too often, "the other" is a casualty in our self-protective quest.

Q6. "We believe that living as mere consumers can create disordered lives out of proportion with the wider needs of the world around us." How has this "consumer mentality" crept into the life of the church?

People often speak of "church shopping," or say things like the "rector's sermons don't feed me." Youth ministry, we now believe, needs to be entertaining and grumbles often abound if the worship "service" exceeds an hour. People who pledge expect a certain amount of "services to be rendered" in return. But increasingly the call to lose our lives for Jesus is absent from our conversations. There is no one to blame for this. It is just a current reality for the twenty-first-century church. It will be helpful to direct the conversation in a way that encourages brainstorming on how we might address the challenge, rather than blaming those who we imagine created it, and begin reimagining what it might mean to live more faithfully.

Q7. "In the Episcopal Church there are two Gospel Sacraments: one is the Eucharist and one is Baptism." In what ways have these two Sacraments shaped your own formation as an Episcopalian?

The leader might ask people about their experience of Baptism and Confirmation and their particular belief on the merits of infant baptism versus adult baptism. Also, special attention might be given to the parallels between what happens to the Eucharistic bread and what we are "signing up for" when we receive it—namely, that like the bread, God's gathered people are "taken and blessed" to be "broken and given" to the world as THE Body of Christ. Such is why Holy Communion is not for "solace only" but also "for strength" and not for "pardon only" but also "renewal." Eucharist is our strength and means of renewal to be sent out into the world on mission.

Q8. Doyle closes this chapter by challenging us to embrace a call to interdependence, as opposed to independence. Do you agree that interdependence is better than independence? If so, what might this mean for the Church?

This is where it is good to be reminded that independence is a Western illusion. The Church is a Body of many parts. We are interdependent and when one part suffers we all do. Thus, the choice for interdependence is always a choice to align ourselves with reality itself. God, by definition, is Interdependent. There is no Father apart from the Father's love for His Son, and no love is made manifest apart from God's Spirit. To say that like God we are both one and many means that we are interdependent.

V. Optional Supplementary Material: The Ministry and Sacraments
Excerpt from Catechism
The Book of Common Prayer
See pages 855-858

The Ministry

Q. Who are the ministers of the Church?

A. The ministers of the Church are lay persons, bishops, priests, and deacons.

Q. What is the ministry of the laity?

A. The ministry of lay persons is to represent Christ and his

Church; to bear witness to him wherever they may be; and, according to the gifts given them, to carry on Christ's work of reconciliation in the world; and to take their place in the life, worship, and governance of the Church.

Q. What is the ministry of a bishop?
A. The ministry of a bishop is to represent Christ and his Church, particularly as apostle, chief priest, and pastor of a diocese; to guard the faith, unity, and discipline of the whole Church; to proclaim the Word of God; to act in Christ's name for the reconciliation of the world and the building up of the Church; and to ordain others to continue Christ's ministry.

Q. What is the ministry of a priest or presbyter?
A. The ministry of a priest is to represent Christ and his Church, particularly as pastor to the people; to share with the bishop in the overseeing of the Church; to proclaim the Gospel; to administer the sacraments; and to bless and declare pardon in the name of God.

Q. What is the ministry of a deacon?
A. The ministry of a deacon is to represent Christ and his Church, particularly as a servant of those in need; and to assist bishops and priests in the proclamation of the Gospel and the administration of the sacraments.

Q. What is the duty of all Christians?
A. The duty of all Christians is to follow Christ; to come together week by week for corporate worship; and to work, pray, and give for the spread of the kingdom of God.

The Sacraments
What are the sacraments?
A. The sacraments are outward and visible signs of inward and spiritual grace, given by Christ as sure and certain means by which we receive that grace.

Q   What is grace?

A.   Grace is God's favor toward us, unearned and
      undeserved; by grace God forgives our sins, enlightens
      our minds, stirs our hearts, and strengthens our wills.

Q   What are the two great sacraments of the Gospel?

A.   The two great sacraments given by Christ to his Church are
      Holy Baptism and the Holy Eucharist.

Discussion Questions:

1. *Would you rank the five sacraments with a little "s" as inferior to
    Baptism and Eucharist? Why or why not?*
2. *Grace is opposed to earning. Does that mean that grace is also
    opposed to effort? In other words, if grace is about God's work in us,
    what part do we play?*
3. *Lay and ordained alike share a common vocation to "represent
    Christ and His Church." What does that mean?*

VI. Conclusion—5 minutes

Reader A reading from the first letter of Paul to the Corinthians.

For just as the body is one and has many members, and all the members
of the body, though many, are one body, so it is with Christ. For in the one
Spirit we were all baptized into one body—Jews or Greeks, slaves or free—
and we were all made to drink of one Spirit. Indeed, the body does not
consist of one member but of many. If the foot were to say, "Because I am
not a hand, I do not belong to the body," that would not make it any less a
part of the body. And if the ear were to say, "Because I am not an eye, I do
not belong to the body," that would not make it any less a part of the body.
If the whole body were an eye, where would the hearing be? If the whole
body were hearing, where would the sense of smell be? But as it is, God
arranged the members in the body, each one of them, as he chose. If all
were a single member, where would the body be? As it is, there are many
members, yet one body.

— 1 Corinthians 12: 12-20

Free intercessions and thanksgivings

The Lord's Prayer

Leader

O God the Father of our Lord Jesus Christ, our only Savior, the Prince of Peace: Give us grace seriously to lay to heart the great dangers we are in by our unhappy divisions; take away all hatred and prejudice, and whatever else may hinder us from godly union and concord; that, as there is but one Body and one Spirit, one hope of our calling, one Lord, one Faith, one Baptism, one God and Father of us all, so we may be all of one heart and of one soul, united in one holy bond of truth and peace, of faith and charity, and may with one mind and one mouth glorify *thee*; through Jesus Christ our Lord. *Amen.*

– BCP 818, A Collect for the Unity of the Church

Session Six
Common Themes & Essential Foundations in Marriage, Part I

I.   Approach—5 minutes

Leader   You send forth your Spirit, and they are created;
People   and so you renew the face of the earth.
                – Psalm 104:31

Reader   A reading from the Letter of Paul to the
                Ephesians:

Husbands, love your wives, as Christ loved the church and gave himself up for her, in order to make her holy by cleansing her with the washing of water by the word, so as to present the church to himself in splendor, without a spot or wrinkle or anything of the kind—yes, so that she may be holy and without blemish. In the same way, husbands should love their wives as they do their own bodies. He who loves his wife loves himself. For no one ever hates his own body, but he nourishes and tenderly cares for it, just as Christ does for the church, because we are members of his body. For this reason a man will leave his father and mother and be joined to his wife, and the two will become one flesh. This is a great mystery, and I am applying it to Christ and the church.

                                        – Ephesians 5:25-32

Silent Reflection

Leader Let us pray…

O gracious and ever living God, you have created us male and female in your image: look mercifully upon each man and woman who come to you seeking your blessing, and assist them with your grace, that with true fidelity and steadfast love they may honor and keep the promises and vows they make; through Jesus Christ our Savior, who lives and reigns with you and the unity of the Holy Spirit, one God, for ever and ever. *Amen.*

                        – adapted from the Collect for Marriage, BCP p. 425

Getting on Board Question—8 minutes

What has been your experience of marriage and family life?

Introduction—2 minutes

This session will look at the origins of marriage in both the Old and New Testaments. The covenant of marriage developed over time as practices varied throughout biblical times. Polygamy was often practiced both by patriarchs and kings. Monogamy emerged as the norm during the first century in both Hebrew and Roman cultures, although there was always a variety of sexual practices and relationships.

Chapter three includes thoughts about the foundations of marriage. Bishop Doyle quotes Charles Price and Louis Weil from their book, *Liturgy for Living*:

The story of creation in the first chapter of Genesis puts an extraordinarily high value on human sexuality. We read, "God created man in his own image, in the image of God he created him; male and female he created them" (Genesis 1:27). Sexual union is created to be one means by which human beings realize and participate in the image of God. (It is not the only one, to be sure. Marriage is not necessary to salvation.) Sexuality is therefore a matter of greatest concern of the Christian faith.

On the other hand, what is designated to be a great good is often, in sin-ridden human life, a source of evil and distortion. The corruption of the best is the worst, as a familiar proverb puts it. Our sexuality is no exception. It brings soaring joy. It can also bring frustration and bitterness. In the biblical understanding of the conditions of human existence after the Fall, the relationship between man and woman comes under the curse, which affects all things. What was designed as a blessing and as expression of deepest human mutuality becomes time and time again, a frustration and an opportunity for one partner to dominate the other. "...Your desire shall be for your husband, and he shall rule over you," the Genesis account reads (3:16).

Under these circumstances, the understanding of marriage in Israel grew with the developing knowledge of God's ways with his people. It came to be recognized that the sexual bond between husband and wife was most secure, satisfying and fulfilling when it was maintained in the context of a relationship marked by the kind of loyalty and faithfulness which God showed to Israel.

– Liturgy for Living pp. 250-251

Discussion of Study Questions—25 minutes

Q1. Bishop Doyle outlines six essential points about marriage (pp. 60-61). What do you think distinguishes Christian marriage from other marriages?

Marriages may be conducted outside the church without a blessing. These marriages are recognized by the church as valid.

Q2. In what ways do you believe Christian marriage is an icon of God's *hesed* or steadfast love for his people?

"Hesed" is the Hebrew word for steadfast love. Paul uses the word "agape" when he speaks of divine love.

Q3. In your opinion how does Genesis set a pattern for marriage?

Both Paul (in Ephesians) and Jesus (in Mark) quote Genesis 2:24, "Therefore a man leaves his father and mother and clings to his wife, and they become one flesh."

Q4. How does secular marriage today depart from your understanding of marriage?

Our understanding of marriage as a lifelong covenant between one man and one woman is being challenged today.

Q5. How do you understand Paul's teaching that the sacred bond of marriage reflects the relationship between Christ and the church?

See Ephesians 5:32: "This is a great mystery, and I am applying it to Christ and the church."

Optional Supplementary Material

The Catechism in the *Book of Common Prayer* defines marriage as a sacramental rite.

Q. What is Holy Matrimony?
A. Holy Matrimony is Christian marriage, in which the woman and man enter into a lifelong union, make their vows before God and the Church, and receive the grace and blessing of God to help them fulfill their vows.
– BCP, p. 861

Marion Hatchett provides a historical background to the development of the sacrament of marriage in his *Commentary on the American Prayer Book.*

In most societies, when persons approach marriage, a series of rites separates them from their peers (the unmarried men and women of the community), prepares them for marriage, and integrates them into the life, responsibilities, and customs of married couples in the community.

Among the Jews the rites of marriage involved a ceremony of betrothal, some time prior to the wedding, in which the father of the bride gave his consent to the union. The wedding itself was preceded by a procession of the bridegroom and friends to the bride's home. She was richly dressed, wearing a veil, which she would not remove until her entry into the bridal chamber.

The ceremony included vows and a written contract ("covenant"), and a blessing over a cup of wine. During the ceremony the bride and groom stood under a canopy in the presence of at least ten witnesses (the "minyan," a minimum number necessary for a synagogue service). Following the ceremony the wedding company went in procession to the bridegroom's home while the witnesses sang songs (see Psalm 45 and the Song of Songs); there was dancing and a feast that lasted from seven to fourteen days.

There is no hint concerning a Christian marriage rite in the New Testament, although it does provide teachings concerning the duties of husbands and wives, parents and children, and married couples within the community. Probably the rites of Judaism were followed with little modification since they were a part of ancient and familiar custom.

Among the pagan Romans, wedding rites began with a betrothal at the home of the bride, where a contract was signed before witnesses. The man gave a betrothal present, kissed the bride, and placed a ring on the fourth finger on her left hand as a symbol of possession. The hands of the two were joined. A banquet followed. Sometime later, on the day of the wedding, the bride was arrayed in her wedding garments, which included a cincture (a symbol of virginity), a yellow dress, flame-colored veil, and floral gown. The bride and groom made a solemn declaration before witnesses after which the pronuba ([a married woman] representing Juno, the goddess of marriage, domesticity, and childbearing) joined their hands. The couple offered a sacrifice at the family altar to propitiate the lares [household gods], and the auspex nuptiarum (priest of the marriage rite) recited a prayer, which the couple repeated as they processed around the altar. At some point the veil or pall was held over the couple. A banquet followed, lasting until nightfall when the bride was led to her new home, accompanied by virgins and young unmarried men singing wedding songs, and was carried over the threshold by her husband. They lit the hearth fire together and she was sprinkled with water, a symbol of fertility among other things.

The pronuba prepared the marriage bed as the couple went through the rites of loosening the marriage cincture and praying to the gods of marriage. On the following day the bride received her new relatives and sacrificed to the gods of her new home.

Incidental references to marriage in the writings of the church fathers indicate that the rites were not radically different among early Christians, except for evidence of the consent and possibly the attendance of the bishop who participated in some marriages. Christian prayers and blessings were, of course, substituted for pagan ones, and a Eucharist replaced the pagan sacrifices.

--Commentary on the American Prayer Book, pp. 427-8

Discussion Questions

1. What are the differences and similarities to marriage today with those in the ancient world?

2. How have you experienced weddings that you and your family have attended?

Conclusion – 5 minutes

Reader A reading from the Letter to the Colossians.

As God's chosen ones, holy and beloved, clothe yourselves with compassion, kindness, humility, meekness, and patience. Bear with one another and, if anyone has a complaint against another, forgive each other;

just as the Lord has forgiven you, so you also must forgive. Above all, clothe yourselves with love, which binds everything together in perfect harmony. And let the peace of Christ rule in your hearts, to which indeed you were called in the one body. And be thankful.

--Colossians 3:12-15

Free intercessions and thanksgivings

The Lord's Prayer

Leader Let us pray together:

Eternal God, author of harmony and happiness, we thank you for the gift of marriage in which men and women seek fulfillment, companionship, and the blessing of family life.

Give patience to those who look forward to marriage.

Give courage to those who face trials within their marriage. Give comfort to those whose marriages are broken. Give gratitude to those whose marriages are successful and fruitful, and let their lives reflect your love and your glory, through Jesus Christ our Lord. *Amen.*

--Michael Saward, Contemporary Parish Prayers, p. 22

Session Seven
Common Themes & Essential Foundations in Traditional Marriage, Part II

Approach – 5 Minutes

Leader Bless the Lord, O my soul;
People O Lord my God, how excellent is your greatness!
 You are clothed with majesty and splendor.

--Psalm 104:1

Reader   A reading from the Gospel of Mark:
But Jesus said to them, "Because of your hardness of heart he (Moses) wrote this commandment for you. But from the beginning of creation, 'God made them male and female." "For this reason a man shall leave his father and mother and be joined to his wife, and the two shall become one flesh' So they are no longer two, but one flesh. Therefore what God has joined together, let no one separate."

----Mark 10:5-9

Silence for reflection

Leader Let us pray....

We thank you, O Lord our God, that the life which we now live in Christ is part of the life eternal, and the fellowship which we have in him unites your whole Church on earth and in heaven; and we pray that as we journey through the years we may know the joys which are without end, and at last come to that abiding city where you live and reign for evermore. *Amen.*

Getting on Board Question—8 minutes

In the reading above, Jesus responded to a question about divorce posed by the Pharisees. What do you believe he was saying about the purpose and sanctity of marriage?

Introduction—2 minutes

In this section of Chapter III, Bishop Doyle discusses the lifelong commitment of marriage. However, divorce is a reality that goes back to Jesus' day. Divorce and remarriage are common today. The paper includes a section on "Remarriage – Making Room for the Pastoral in the Midst of Reality."

In 1973 the General Convention removed the canonical prohibition against the remarriage of members of the Church whose former spouse was still living, and whose prior marriage was valid from its inception. The provision that most of us take for granted today was a long, painful development. It took over 177 years for the Church to make up its mind about the nature of remarriage and how it would deal with an emerging growth in divorces among its members. These were not only discussion and division on canon law.

We as a Church came to an understanding that when individuals in a marriage no longer embrace the whole other person through a mutual love, or recognize their partners as God's creation, or treat one another with dignity, or as fully human, or through the appreciation of each other's beauty, or by living out symbolically the nature of the Trinity, such marriages are dissolved.

IV. Discussion of Study Questions—25 minutes

Bishop Doyle concludes this section of his paper with the following thoughts:

Today marriage and remarriage are regular parts of our life as a church. The Episcopal Church in the Diocese of Texas did 101 remarriages in 2011 alone. That is a lot in my opinion. In point of fact, a number of those were third marriages.

Because it is a part of our common life today, we may forget that in the Scriptures Jesus speaks particularly against this, as do the Epistles. In fact, there is more in the New Testament Scripture against remarriage than there is on other sexual exploits. I say this because we all have our own canon of scripture. I mean by this that we typically, in an ever-human way, seek to make our argument out of scripture that we know. We should be aware that the Church has changed its mind on divorce and remarriage considerably since the time of Jesus. Yet, I would offer we did so out of pastoral concern and desire to offer redeeming grace to those who sought relief from marriages they believed failed and an ever-new opportunity for transformation through the gift of marriage. We as a church have come to believe that remarriage (though clearly against scripture) mirrors God's own unconditional love.

Q1. How do you grapple with divorce and remarriage in light of Jesus' teaching?

In Mark 10:11-12 and Luke 16:18, Jesus states that divorce and remarriage is adulterous, with no exception. In Matthew 5:32 one exception is made in the case of "unchastity."

Q2. Under what circumstances do you believe divorce is permissible?

There are several grounds for divorce such as: abandonment, cruelty, insanity and others. Many speak of the death of the relationship or that the marriage is irretrievably broken down.

Q3. How would you respond to someone who wants to remarry after a divorce?

The church allows for remarriage after one or both parties are divorced. A period of time for healing and counseling is recommended before we permit marriages to receive the blessing of the church.

Q4. How can your congregation be an instrument of healing for adults and children experiencing divorce?

Marriages are contracted within the community of the church. Consider how we can be supportive of couples and families going through divorce.

Q5. How does "remarriage offer hope for a renewed commitment and covenant between two people who have let go of a previous life commitment?"

Optional Supplementary Material

John Stott writes a section on Marriage and Divorce in *Issues Facing Christians Today*.

The higher our concept of God's original ideal for marriage and the family, the more devastating the experience of divorce is bound to be. A marriage which began with tender love and rich expectations now lies in ruins. Marital breakdown is always a tragedy. It contradicts God's will, frustrates his purpose, brings to husband and wife the acute pains of alienation, disillusion, recrimination and guilt, and precipitates in any children of the marriage a crisis of bewilderment, insecurity and often anger.

He continues with a section on the Covenant Principle.

There is much in the covenant model of marriage which is compelling. To begin with, it is a thoroughly biblical notion. It also emphasizes the great solemnity both of covenant making and of covenant breaking—in the former case emphasizing love, commitment, public recognition, exclusive faithfulness and sacrifice, and in the latter the sin of going back on promises and rupturing a relationship of love. I confess, however, that my problem is how to fuse the two concepts of covenant loyalty and matrimonial offence. I can understand reasons for not wanting to build permission to divorce on two offences. But if Scripture regards the marriage covenant of being broken in several ways, how shall we explain the single offence mentioned in our Lord's exceptive clause? Certainly the covenant relationship envisaged in marriage (the 'one flesh union') is far deeper than other covenants, whether a suzerainty treaty, a business deal or even a friendship. May it not be, therefore, that nothing less than a violation (by sexual infidelity) of this fundamental relationship can break the marriage covenant?

It seems to me that we must allow these perspectives of God's covenant to shape our understanding of the marriage covenant. The marriage covenant is not an ordinary human contract which, if one party to it reneges, may be renounced by the other. It is more like God's covenant with his people.

Discussion Questions

1. This is a challenging perspective on the Covenant of Marriage. Do you agree that Jesus was calling us to take seriously the covenant principle in marriage?

2. What is your perspective on the Covenant of Marriage?

Conclusion—5 minutes

Reader   A reading from the First Letter of Paul to the Corinthians.

Love never ends. But as for prophecies, they will come to an end; as for tongues, they will cease; as for knowledge, it will come to an end. For we know only in part, and we prophesy only in part but when the complete comes, the partial will come to an end. When I was a child, I thought like a child, I reasoned like a child; when I became an adult, I put an end to childish ways. For now we see in a mirror dimly, but then we will see face to face. Now I know only in part; then I will know fully, even as I have been fully known. And now faith, hope, and love abide, these three; but the greatest of these is love.

--1 Corinthians 13: 8-13

Free intercessions and thanksgivings

The Lord's Prayer

Leader Let us pray together:

All   O God of peace, you have taught us that in returning and rest we shall be saved, in quietness and confidence shall be our strength; by the might of your Spirit lift us, we pray, to your presence where we may be still and know that you are God; through Jesus Christ our Lord.
Amen.

--BCP, p. 832

Session Eight
Opposing Views

I. Approach—5 minutes

Leader   Oh, how good and pleasant it is;
People   when brethren live together in unity!

--Psalm 133:1

Reader   A reading from Paul's letter to the Philippians.
Let the same mind be in you that was in Christ Jesus, who, though he was in the form of God, did not regard equality with God as something to be exploited, but emptied himself, taking the form of a slave, being born in human likeness. And being found in human form, he humbled himself and became obedient to the point of death – even death on a cross. Therefore God also highly exalted him and gave him the name that is above every name, so that at the name of Jesus every knee should bend, in heaven and on earth and under the earth, and every tongue should confess that Jesus Christ is Lord, to the glory of God the Father.

--Philippians 2: 5-11

Silence for reflection

Leader

Lord Jesus Christ, you said to your apostles, "Peace I give to you; my own peace I leave with you:" Regard not our sins, but the faith of your Church, and give to us the peace and unity of that heavenly City, where with the Father and the Holy Spirit you live and reign, now and forever. *Amen.*

--BCP 395, a Collect for Peace

II. Getting on Board Question—8 minutes

Has your experience of the debate over human sexuality in the Episcopal Church been mostly positive or negative? Why or why not?

III. Introduction—2 minutes

In chapter eight Bishop Doyle looks at the two primary and opposing views of human sexuality that are active in our church. This chapter offers a concise summary of each view. Bishop Doyle ends this chapter by offering some thoughts of his own. He then charges us to find unity in the midst of our differences.

Doyle's first assertion is that the church has been fighting since its inception, a fact he says that few of us seem to grasp. He notes that we are a nostalgic church with "a false sense of our past and our present." It is in this context that Doyle introduces the concept of *adiaphora*, which refers to "things that do not make a difference, matters regarded as non-essential, issues about which one can disagree without dividing the Church." He then quotes *The Windsor Report* at length to expand on the concept of *adiaphora*, and its close cousin, the concept of *subsidiarity*, "the principle that matters in the Church should be decided as close to the local level as possible." He says that the more the concept of adiaphora applies to an issue, the more the concept of subsidiarity should also apply. Put differently, issues that are not central to the church's mission should be dealt with at the local level. Doyle's purpose in introducing the concepts of adiaphora and subsidiarity is to frame the debate over human sexuality in the church. Our problem is that *both sides* of the human sexuality debate deem the issue to not be adiaphora – they just take different sides! Doyle then takes his stand by reasserting his position behind this paper. "A shared unanimity by all individual members of the Church is neither possible nor necessary for unity in mission."

Doyle then turns his attention to summarizing two papers written by various theological camps in the House of Bishops. One paper summarizes the traditionalist stance on marriage. The second paper summarizes the more liberal perspective on same sex blessings. Doyle first summarizes the traditionalist paper, which asserts that same sex relationships are not part of God's intent in creation. The traditionalists assert that the approval of same sex covenants comes "more from assimilation to modern culture than from following Jesus in learning how better to understand and live by the Scriptures."

The progressive paper is much different. They argue that marriage is primarily a discipline whereby God dispenses grace to sinners. Since the mission of the church is "to offer grace to sinful people and inspire virtue through a covenant with one another and with God," gays and lesbians must be included in that process. Furthermore, the progressives reference many instances in the New Testament whereby the Spirit leads God's people to do something "new" that many opposed at the time on the basis of how they read scripture, such as the inclusion of Gentiles, abolishing circumcision and the Old Testament dietary laws. The progressives do not call for an end to disagreement, however, "for that is part of the labor of our common baptism into God's mission."

Doyle closes chapter four by offering his thoughts on the two arguments. His primary conclusion is that "they are very different and run almost on different rails of the Anglican tradition." Doyle goes as far as to say that the two sides are having separate conversations altogether. Doyle does this not to criticize, but to be clear that "the two divergent sides will not meet in the middle." This chasm in the conversation is the essence of our struggle. Our response must be to "find a Christian unity beyond this difference and continue our missionary work of proclaiming the Gospel in spite of our difference and the gulf that appears before our beloved Church."

IV. Discussion of Study Questions—25 minutes

Q1. What in this chapter strikes or impresses you, either positively or negatively?

Q2. Bishop Doyle asserts that "we have a nostalgic sense that somehow we have never really fought over things before, or that somehow we were unified up until just recently." Do you agree with his assessment?

The leader might remind the group that much of the New Testament was written to respond to conflicts that emerged in the early church. Furthermore, differing views on many matters were tolerated and encouraged. To quote St. Paul, "Let each be convinced in his own mind." (Rom 14:5) Interesting New Testament examples of conflict might be cited, such as Paul's showdown with Peter in Galatians 2, or the fight that broke out when Hellenistic widows were being neglected in the daily distribution of food in Acts 6. Many credit that fight in particular with the development of the diaconate, which might lend itself to the viewpoint that God can use conflict to develop and strengthen the Church.

Q3. Bishop Doyle introduces the term *adiaphora* to refer to issues of doctrine or practice that we can disagree on because they do not make a difference to being faithful to the Gospel. Can you name one aspect of church life (other than human sexuality) that you deem to be *adiaphora,* and one that you do not?

It will be good for the leader to have many examples handy. Non-adiaphora items might include reading scripture in the context of worship. Adiaphora items might include the color of the altar hangings or whether contemporary or traditional music is used in the context of worship. The leader might also remind the group that our struggle in the church is that both sides of the human sexuality debate deem marriage to not be adiaphora. If we all thought it was adiaphora, we wouldn't have a problem in the first place.

Q4. Which of the following would you consider *adiaphora?*

military service, the resurrection of the body, human trafficking, recycling

Most Episcopalians would consider the decision to serve in the military, or to register for the draft, an instance of adiaphora. Though a weighty issue, both sides are within the Christian, and even within the Anglican, tent. The resurrection of the body is not adiaphora because the belief is an article in the Creeds. Human trafficking is not adiaphora because it violates the Ten Commandments and the Baptismal Covenant and is dehumanizing. Like most Christians, Anglicans regard recycling as good and could find for it biblical or theological justifications but they would not feel the need to break communion or "disfellowship" someone who does not recycle. Therefore, it too is adiaphora.

Q5. "It is important to listen to the views of our neighbor if we are to understand where we are as a church and to understand where others stand." Why is it so hard to listen to the view of our neighbor, especially when her view differs from our own?

Our brains are hard-wired to respond to "threats." Even though we would never admit that someone thinking differently than us is a real threat to our wellbeing, our habitual ways of acting signal our brain to (mistakenly) believe that differing views pose a threat to us. As a result, most of us craft responses while we listen to other people. Our goal in listening is not to understand but to win, or at least not lose; to look good, or at least not look bad. The effect of this is that we rarely listen at all. Real listening is a skill that takes work and practice. We must believe that listening matters and that St. Paul was correct in saying "we see only in part" (1 Cor 13:12). But listening well is an important skill to develop. "If anyone has ears to hear, let him hear." (Mark 4:23)

Q6. What is your best understanding of the traditionalist perspective? In what ways did their argument surprise you?

The leader might remind the group that their argument is more nuanced than "the Bible says being gay is a sin." Their primary argument is that Jesus interpreted the Torah in terms of God's intention for humanity in creation. Jesus is stricter on divorce than the Old Testament, for example, because Moses allowed divorce as a concession for people's hardness of heart. What may surprise readers is that the traditionalists invite people to look for genuine errors in their thinking. They also remind their readers that both sides are inflating the role of marriage in the grand scheme of God's vast redemption purposes.

Q7. What is your best understanding of the liberal perspective? In what ways did their argument surprise you?

The leader might highlight that the liberals, more so than the traditionalists, are emphasizing our common sinfulness. Their argument depends upon all of us being sinful as marriage is a means whereby God offers sinful people grace, which is the mission of the church. It is also worth noting that the expansionist view does not call for an end to disagreement, but celebrates our disagreement on this issue as evidence of the strong bonds of our common baptism.

Q8. Doyle says that finding some middle ground between these two arguments is impossible because two different conversations are taking place. Do you find the church's gridlock discouraging or encouraging?

It is obvious that most, at first, will be discouraged. But, gridlock is our reality and this paper is a response to our gridlock on this issue. Furthermore, Bishop Doyle's purpose in writing is to encourage us. The leader might find it helpful to highlight that both arguments are faithful to the Anglican tradition, which is a testament to the depth and vastness of our tradition. This is something to celebrate. In addition, telling the truth about the impossibility of meeting in the middle is a necessary step to moving forward.

Q9. "You and I must find a Christian unity beyond this difference and continue our missionary work of proclaiming the Gospel in spite of our differences and the gulf that appears before our beloved Church." How might this exhortation be lived out in your own life, or in the life of your congregation?

There are many answers to this subjective question. But some good answers might include fostering a greater respect for people who see marriage differently, or learning to celebrate the vastness of our Anglican heritage, or perhaps redirecting our focus from sexuality to mission.

V. Optional Supplementary Material

Excerpt from Thomas Merton's writing
New Seeds of Contemplation
Ch. 10 "A Body of Broken Bones"

In the whole world, throughout the whole history, even among religious men and among saints, Christ suffers dismemberment.

All over the face of the earth the avarice and lust of men breed unceasing divisions among them, and the wounds that tear men from union with one another widen and open out into huge wars. Murder, massacres, revolution, hatred, the slaughter and torture of the bodies and souls of men, the destruction of cities by fire, the starvation of millions, the annihilation of populations and finally the cosmic inhumanity of atomic war: Christ is massacred in His members, torn limb from limb; God is murdered in men.

The history of the world, with the material destruction of cities and nations and people, expressed the interior division that tyrannizes the souls of all men, and even of the saints. Even the innocent, even those in whom Christ lives by charity, even those who want with their whole heart to love one another, remain divided and separate. Although they are already one in Him, their union is hidden from them, because it still only possesses the secret substance of their souls.

But their minds and their judgments and their desires, their human characters and faculties, their appetites and their ideals are all imprisoned in the slag of an inescapable egotism which pure love has not yet been able to refine.

As long as we are on earth, the love that unites us will bring us suffering by our very contact with one another, because this love is the resetting of a Body of broken bones.

Even saints cannot live with saints on this earth without some anguish, without some pain at the differences that come between them.

There are two things which men can do about the pain of disunion with other men. They can love or they can hate.

Discussion Questions:

1. Merton uses strong language in saying, "God is murdered in men." What do you think he means by that?
2. "Love," Merton says, "is the resetting of broken bones." How does this statement speak to the gridlock we currently are experiencing over issues of human sexuality?
3. Merton suggests that we can only choose love or hate and that there isn't an in-between. Do you agree? What does it mean to choose love?

VI. Conclusion—5 minutes

Reader A reading from the first letter of Paul to the Corinthians.

Now I appeal to you, brothers and sisters, by the name of our Lord Jesus Christ, that all of you should be in agreement and that there should be no divisions among you, but that you should be united in the same mind and the same purpose. For it has been reported to me by Chloe's people that there are quarrels among you, my brothers and sisters. What I mean is that each of you says, 'I belong to Paul', or 'I belong to Apollos', or 'I belong to Cephas', or 'I belong to Christ.' Has Christ been divided? Was Paul crucified for you? Or were you baptized in the name of Paul?

--1 Corinthians 1: 10-13

Free intercessions and thanksgivings

The Lord's Prayer

Leader Let us pray together:

All Almighty and everlasting God, you have given to us your servants grace, by the confession of a true faith, to acknowledge the glory of the eternal Trinity, and in the power of your divine Majesty to worship the Unity: Keep us steadfast in this faith and worship, and bring us at last to see you in your one and eternal glory, O Father; who with the Son and the Holy Spirit live and reign, one God, for ever and ever. *Amen.*

--BCP 228, A Collect for Trinity Sunday

Session Nine
A Strategy for Unity in Mission

I.   Approach—5 minutes

Leader   Not to us, O Lord, not to us, but to your Name
            give glory;
People   because of your love and because of your
            faithfulness.

--Psalm 115: 1

Reader   A reading from the Letter of Paul to the Ephesians.

I therefore, the prisoner of the Lord, beg you to lead a life worthy of the calling to which you have been called, with all humility and gentleness, with patience, bearing with one another in love, making every effort to maintain the unity of Spirit in the bond of peace. There is one body and one Spirit, just as you were called to the one hope of your calling, one Lord, one faith, one baptism, one God and Father of all, who is above all, and through all and in all.

--Ephesians 4:1-6

Silence for reflection

Leader Let us pray…

O God, by whom the meek are guided in judgment, and light rises up in darkness for the godly: Grant us, in all our doubts and uncertainties, the grace to ask what you would have us to do, that the Spirit of wisdom may save us from all false choices, and that in your light we may see light, and in your straight path may not stumble; through Jesus Christ our Lord. *Amen.*

--BCP p. 832, A Prayer for Guidance

II.   Getting on Board Question—8 minutes

Tell about a time when you were responsible for negotiating a difficult settlement between opposing people or parties.

III.   Introduction—2 minutes

Chapter VI details a strategy for the bishop to authorize the Blessing of Same Sex Couples as well as provides traditional options for parishes which do not wish to bless relationships outside marriage.

By way of further introduction, Bishop Doyle made these comments in a press release at the time *Unity in Mission* was published:

"I hold our work for the Lord Jesus Christ to be paramount in who we are and in everything we do. Our mission and ministry have been dogged by our disagreements and conflict over the blessing of same-sex couples for too long at the expense of the mission of the gospel. I pray that this plan will help to guide us beyond conflict and give us the ability to refocus our attention on the hurting world around us. I am hopeful that we will learn from one another and deepen our respect and love for one another through this process."

IV.   Discussion of Study Questions—25 minutes

Q1. Bishop Doyle claims that his strategy "is not a move towards congregationalism." What is congregationalism? How can he make this claim? Do you agree?

Congregationalism is a system of church governance that leaves legislative and disciplinary functions to the individual congregations. The Bishop is simply allowing congregations on this particular issue to choose among options which he has clearly defined, in accord with the canons and resolutions of The Episcopal Church.

Q3. How does the strategy safeguard the position of traditional congregations within the Episcopal Church?

The resolution passed at General Convention 2012 and 2015 requires that congregations using the rite receive the approval of the diocesan bishop, so the bishop is given the power whether or not to allow the blessings to take place.

Traditional and progressive congregations are allowed to affirm their position

Q5. Note the following comment by Bishop Doyle:
The solution to this impasse shall be my reliance on our polity, canons and structure, which already make room for clergy to have local liturgical freedom and parishes to self-differentiate given their local mission contexts.

What approach is being taken in your congregation, diocese or province regarding the blessing of same-sex relationships? Do you believe that this is the appropriate approach for your people?

Q6. What have you and your group gained from this study? What is important to you as you reflect on this study?

V.   Optional Supplementary Material

You may read the word of Standing Commission on Liturgy and Music and the Resolution passed at General Convention – 2012 on the following website:
http://episcopalarchives.org/SCLM/

To watch a video of how one congregation discussed whether or not to celebrate same-sex blessing go to:
http://www.youtube.com/watch?v=AIw2BCDA2Yw

Discussion Questions
1. What questions arise for you after watching this video?
2. In what positive ways did the congregation come to a consensus?

VI.   Conclusion—5 minutes

Reader A reading from the Gospel of John.

I give you a new commandment, that you love one another as I have loved you, you also should love one another. By this everyone will know that you are my disciples, if you have love for one another.

--John 13:34-35

Free Intercessions and thanksgivings

The Lord's Prayer

Leader Let us pray together:

All Gracious Father, we pray for your holy Catholic Church. Fill it with all truth, in all truth with all peace. Where it is corrupt, purify it; where it is in error, direct it; where in any thing it is amiss, reform it. Where it is right, strengthen it; where it is in want provide for it; where it is divided, reunite it; for the sake of Jesus Christ your Son our Savior. *Amen.*

--BCP p. 816, a Prayer for the Church

11 FORWARD INTO MISSION

In the last hours before His Passion, Jesus turned to the unity and mission of His disciples. In fact, Jesus clearly connected the two—"...that they become completely one, so that the world may know..."

Charles Swindoll offers some food for thought on our struggle for unity in the midst of differing opinions. "Union has an affiliation with others but no common bond that makes them one in heart. Uniformity has everyone looking and thinking alike. Unanimity is complete agreement across the board. Unity, however, refers to a oneness of heart, a similarity of purpose and an agreement on major points of doctrine."[146]

For at least forty years the Anglican Communion has been embroiled in conflict around issues of human sexuality. That conflict has been all the more intense because it emerges from divergent views of Scripture, tradition and reason that are held sincerely and passionately by members of our Communion. From a posture of "win-lose" it has often seemed that the only possible solution is an all or nothing approach: "You either agree with my position on this issue or we need to part company." And that, indeed, has sometimes seemed to be the strategy of those on every side of this highly sensitive and often emotional issue.

The church has paid a high price for the conflict. The loss of membership in The Episcopal Church over the same period of time is both frightening and disheartening. It may be an oversimplification to attribute the loss of membership to a single issue; there are many factors involved. But there is no question that people have been hurt, people have felt abandoned by their church, people have been left spiritually bereft, and many have "unplugged" out of exhaustion. The real casualty has been, and continues to be, the mission of the gospel of Jesus Christ. The real casualty is represented by countless lives left without the hope of the Word of God.

We are called to a higher standard of community relationships built upon reconciliation over division. Our response to an issue that has caused such strife is neither a cause to celebrate or grieve, nor to claim "win" or "loss" for any "side" in this ongoing struggle but it is an opportunity.

We have an opportunity to celebrate our authentic Anglican heritage of finding solutions that transcend our inevitable differences over certain aspects of the Christian life, and to celebrate authentic diversity by moving beyond our divisions over these issues toward our mission which can, and must ultimately, unite us.[147]

So often we are quick to chose scripture that we want to defend or use to tell others how they are supposed to live their lives. It is time for the church to chose Jesus' own prayer for us as a core scripture worth holding up against our lives.

> *I ask not only on behalf of these, but also on behalf of those who will believe in me through their word, that they may all be one. As you, Father, are in me and I am in you, may they also be in us, so that the world may believe that you have sent me. The glory that you have given me I have given them, so that they may be one, as we are one, I in them and you in me, that they may become completely one, so that the world may know that you have sent me and have loved them even as you have loved me.* (John 17:20-23)

ABOUT THE AUTHOR

The Rt. Rev. C. Andrew Doyle, the ninth Bishop of the Episcopal Diocese of Texas, summarizes his autobiography in six words: "Met Jesus on pilgrimage; still walking." He and his wife JoAnne live in Houston with their daughters. He is author of *Unabashedly Episcopalian: Proclaiming the Good News of the Episcopal Church* and *Church: A Generous Community Amplified for the Future.*

---

[1] The Rev. Dr. Russell Levenson, "Reclothing the Emperor," The Living Church, July 15, 2011.

[2] Ibid.

[3] The Rev. Dr. Zahl does tell us that Philip Wylie was an awful writer by today's standards, and that his attitude is often holier than thou. Nevertheless, from smoking to the Internet, Zahl challenges the listener to see that the redactions in Wylie's work are mostly true, incorporating a list of works that stretch from 1928 to 1971, including the book *When Worlds Collide*.

[4] The Rev. Dr. Paul Zahl, PZ Podcast, Episode #59. http://www.mbird.com/2011/08/pzs-podcast-should-i-stay-or-should-i-go/

[5] The Anglican Way: The Significance of the Episcopal Office for the Communion of the Church, [TSEO] Inter-Anglican Theological and Doctrinal Commission, October 2007, 12ff. See also the Book of Common Prayer [BCP]. (Church Publishing: New York, 1979) 517ff.

[6] BCP, 521.

[7] Philippians 3:10

END NOTES

[8] BCP, 517.

[9] BCP, 518.

[10] BCP, 517ff.

[11] Brian MacClaren, *Forward,* in Ken Howard's *Paradoxy: Creating Christian Community beyond Us and Them* (Paraclete Press, 2010)x.

[12] TSEO.

[13] I take the definition of reconciliation repeated often by my friends the Very Rev. John Whitcombe and Canon David Porter, who use this definition in their own work of reconciliation throughout the world as ambassadors of the Community of the Cross of Nails.

[14] TSEO.

[15] TSEO, 12ff. See also BCP, 518

[16] Ibid. See also BCP, 518.

[17] TSEO.

[18] BCP, 517 and 518

[19] BCP, 518

[20] Collect for Richard Hooker: O God of truth and peace, you raised up your servant Richard Hooker in a day of bitter controversy to defend with sound reasoning and great charity the catholic and reformed religion. Grant that we may maintain the middle way, not as a compromise for the sake of peace, but

as a comprehension for the sake of truth. Holy Women, Holy Men: Celebrating the Saints (Church Publishing: New York, 2010) 667.

[21] Public Domain and can be found in the Hymnal (Church Publishing: New York, 1982) 525.

[22] I do not imply here a neo-latitudinarianism, for I believe this freedom is only manifest within a community that proclaims a monotheistic faith in God as creator and Jesus as the incarnate Son who fulfills salvation history.

[23] Romans 14: 4-5, 22

[24] 1 Corinthians 1:18

[25] The Anglican Way: Signposts on a Common Journey, (The Working Party on Theological Education[TEAC], May 2007) 2.

[26] TEAC, 2.

[27] Primates are the heads of each Provincial Church in the Communion, Ibid.

[28] BCP, 855; see also 861ff.

[29] BCP, 853.

[30] TEAC, 4.

[31] The Windsor Report, ¶34 & 35. The Windsor Report, while not accepted by the Communion officially, is a major masterpiece on the unifying aspects of our common life together as Anglicans.

[32] BCP, Baptism 304; Ordination: Bishop 517, 518, 521 (similar passages may be found throughout ordinal; and Catechism 853.)

[33] TWR, ¶57.

[34] Ibid.

[35] BCP, 864.

[36] TWR, ¶3.

[37] Ibid.

[38] Ibid., ¶5.

[39] TEAC, 6, 7.

[40] TEAC, 6.

[41] TWR, ¶53

[42] Ibid.

[43] TWR, ¶54

[44] TWR, ¶57.

[45] Ibid.

[46] BCP, 304.

[47] BCP, 853.

[48] Ibid.

[49] Ibid.

[50] Ibid.

[51] TEAC, p 8.

[52] Ibid., p 9.

[53] BCP, 857.

[54] TEAC, 9. The TEAC document gives a sense of the Anglican notion of our relationship with God nurtured in worship. They write: "5) Our relationship with God is nurtured through our encounter with the Father, Son and Holy Spirit in word and sacrament. This experience enriches and shapes our understanding of God and our communion with one another. 6) As Anglicans we offer praise to the Triune Holy God, expressed through corporate worship, combining order with freedom. In penitence and thanksgiving we offer ourselves in service to God in the world. Through our liturgies and forms of worship we seek to integrate the rich traditions of the past with the varied cultures of our diverse communities. As broken and sinful persons and communities, aware of our need of God's mercy, we live by grace through faith and continually strive to offer holy lives to God. Forgiven through Christ and strengthened by word and sacrament, we are sent out into the world in the power of the Spirit."

[55] TAW, 11.9.

[56] TAW, 11.10.

[57] TAW, 12.

[58] TEAC, 13.

[59] BCP, 305.

[60] TEAC, 17.

[61] BCP, 857.

[62] The Rev. Dr. Robert Prichard has an excellent paper on the nature of our communion relationship entitled: The Anglican Communion: A Brief History Lesson. You may read it here: http://www.livingchurch.org/anglican-communion-brief-history-lesson.

[63] BCP, 858.

[64] BCP, 360.

[65] Ibid.

[66] R. Runcie, Opening Address reproduced in The Truth Shall Make You Free (The Lambeth Conference, Church House Publishing: London, 1988) 16.

[67] TWR, 37.

[68] As you will see, both remarriage and the blessing of same-sex relationships are recent innovations in our tradition.

[69] I am very appreciative to The Rev. Christopher Bowhay for help on the introduction to this section and his particular support in parsing the theology of the Nuptial Mystery.

[70] Writings on Marriage, [WOM] Greg Jones, et al, Diocese of North Carolina, 2009, 13. I want to acknowledge that here I am dealing with the ideal and theology of marriage. It is important to recognize transparently that there has

been over the years a strong patriarchic message embedded in the Christian and Hebrew scriptures regarding marriage. The treatment of women in Christian marriage has not been positive throughout the history of this secular institution and religious sacrament.

[71] Ibid.

[72] Ibid.

[73] Theology of Christian Marriage, Crossroad Publishing, 1983, 14.

[74] Ibid.

[75] BCP, 423. This was included in the 1662, 1775, 1892, and 1928 BCPs, while omitted from the 1786 and1789-1871 editions.

[76] N. T. Wright, What Is This Word? The incomprehensible, intimate Christmas story. The sermon was republished in *Christianity Today* and it may be read in its entirety here: http://www.christianitytoday.com/ct/2006/decemberweb-only/151-42.0.html?start=1

[77] Mark 2:13-22, or Luke 5:33-39

[78] Wright, What Is This Word?

[79] Ibid.

[80] BCP, 358.

[81] BCP, 429.

[82] Dr. Scott Bader-Saye, private correspondence regarding this paper.

[83] Ibid.

[84]Charles Price and Louis Weil, *Liturgy for Living*, Volume 5 (Seabury Press: New York, 1979).

[85] Ibid, 249.

[86] Ibid.

[87] Ibid.

[88] WOM, 18.

[89] Ibid.

[90] WOM, 18-19.

[91] Moses allowed it because of our sinfulness—our hardness of heart. At the time Jesus spoke, some people believed that the law permitted divorce at any time. The reasons for divorce were not important; as long as there was a legal notice, there could be a divorce. For example, Herod the King divorced his first wife so that he could marry his brother's wife. Herod thought that he had the right to do this. One of the reasons he allegedly arrested John the Baptist was that he opposed him. There were still others in Jesus' day who thought that there could be divorce only because of adultery. The Pharisees wanted Jesus to declare which opinion was right.

[92] WOM, 20.

[93] Ibid.

[94] 2011 Barna study reported one-fifth of young adults with a Christian

background said "church is like a country club, only for insiders" (22%). Six Reason Young Christians Leave the Church, read more here: http://www.barna.org/new-topics/you-lost-me
[95] A 2008 Barna study "showed that the percentage of adults who have been married and divorced varies from segment to segment. For instance, the groups with the most prolific experience of marriage ending in divorce are downscale adults (39%), Baby Boomers (38%), those aligned with a non-Christian faith (38%), African-Americans (36%), and people who consider themselves to be liberal on social and political matters (37%). Among the population segments with the lowest likelihood of having been divorced subsequent to marriage are Catholics (28%), evangelicals (26%), upscale adults (22%), Asians (20%) and those who deem themselves to be conservative on social and political matters (28%). Born-again Christians who are not evangelical were indistinguishable from the national average on the matter of divorce: 33% have been married and divorced. The survey did not determine if the divorce occurred before or after the person had become born again. However, previous research by Barna has shown that less than two out of every ten people who accept Christ as their savior do so after their first marriage. In fact, when evangelicals and non-evangelical born-again Christians are combined into an aggregate class of born-again adults, their divorce figure is statistically identical to that of non-born-again adults: 32% versus 33%, respectively." Read article here: http://www.barna.org/barna-update/article/15-familykids/42-new-marriage-and-divorce-statistics-released
[96] WOM, 21.
[97] WOM, 21.
[98] WOM, 21.
[99] WOM, 21.
[100] Ibid.
[101] Ibid.
[102] WOM, 21.
[103] WOM, 25.
[104] BCP, 423.
[105] Kenneth E. North, "Holy Matrimony, Divorce, and Remarriage According to the Canons of The Episcopal Church." An online article published on the Canon Law Institute website. You can read the article here: http://www.canonlaw.org/article_matrimony.htm.
[106] Ibid.
[107] Ibid.
[108] Ibid.
[109] Ibid.
[110] Ibid.

[111] Ibid.

[112] Ibid.

[113] Ibid.

[114] Windsor Report, Paragraphs 36-37, p 21.

[115] BCP, 430.

[116] Augustine, Letters, 61. Also McKim, 59.

[117] We might remember well that the Donatist controversy, as it emerged and has re-emerged over the years, reveals that the church has often decided that what a person says, and does, will not affect their ministry or the efficacy of their sacramental offerings. During the time of persecution, some Christians handed over sacred texts and worshiped the Roman gods; meanwhile, still others died for their beliefs. The community was divided over the efficacy of the ministry of the traditor, or traitor. The question was about the purity of the ministers and of the church itself. Augustine would eventually enter the fight and argue that the Bible refers to the pure church as the Church that still exists in the kingdom of God. The locus of the point is not the cleric here but that the church has long lived out its ministry and mission in the company of those who were not like-minded. (This is quite the countercultural idea today.) On this earth the church exists as "mixed company," filled with believers of all kinds. So Augustine taught the visible and invisible church, the church today and the church yet to come. For Augustine, the church remained Holy not by the personal virtues of its membership but by the grace of God communicated through the sacrament of baptism and Eucharist. "Baptism belongs to Christ, regardless of who may give it." He continues, "The genuineness and holiness of the sacrament [does not depend upon] what the recipient of the sacrament believes and with what faith he is imbued." We have long lived in a church of diverse opinions both within the clergy and lay order. Donald K. McKim, *Theological Turning Points*, John Knox Press, 1988, 55ff. Augustine, On Baptism, Chapter 3. Also, McKim, 58ff.

[118] The paper was entitled: "Same-Sex Relationships in the Life of the Church" offered by The Theology Committee of the House of Bishops. It may be read in its entirety here: http://www.collegeforbishops.org/resources.

[119] Robert Gagnon in *The Bible and Homosexual Practice: Texts and Hermeneutics* (Nashville: Abingdon, 2001) 71. And, Richard Hays, *The Moral Vision of the New Testament* (San Francisco: HarperCollins, 1996) 381.

[120] House of Bishops' Paper on Sexuality, 15ff.

[121] Andrew Lang has an interesting insight worth mentioning here. Lang is a UCC minister. He writes, "Like heterosexual marriage and celibate community, these relationships are 'schools for sinners,' in which two partners learn how live in the paradox of freedom that is unlimited precisely because it is limite by the other... Neither same-sex relationships nor celibate community are

objectively 'equal' to heterosexual marriage. The marriage between a man and a woman has its own distinctive and privileged character. But neither are they 'second-class' marriages. They are moral relationships and they have a specific claim on the ministry of the church... Same-sex couples therefore have a claim on the pastoral care of the church. The church must not abandon us to the moral disorder of a fallen world that is in rebellion against God. But the church's pastoral concern for these couples necessarily requires the public, liturgical expression of the vows that bind them together." You may read the whole text of his argument here: http://www.ucc.org/beliefs/theology/does-god-have-a-plan-for.html

[122] Ibid.

[123] Ibid.

[124] These texts are also, unless otherwise noted, taken from the House of Bishops' Theological Paper on Marriage.

[125] From the report to the 78th General Convention of the Task Force for the Study of Marriage: https://extranet.generalconvention.org/staff/files/download/12485.pdf

[126] Ibid.

[127] Ibid.

[128] Ibid.

[129] Ibid.

[130] You can find the report here: http://www.generalconvention.org/home/bluebook

[131] McKim, 175ff.

[132] You may read the text in its entirety here: http://www.ssw.edu/conversation-covenant?phpMyAdmin=d82de654bdb95466ba2ba5d15ad452a5.

[133] Ibid.

[134] Ibid.

[135] Ibid.

[136] Ibid.

[137] The Most Rev. and Rt. Hon. Justin Welby, Archbishop of Canterbury, http://www.archbishopofcanterbury.org/pages/reconciliation-.html.

[138] Public Domain.

[139] The Primates Meeting Communique, February 2005, http://www.anglicancommunion.org/media/68387/communique-_english.pdf?year=2005.

[140] You can find the Archbishop's statement here: tp://www.archbishopofcanterbury.org/articles.php/5581/response-to-the-piscopal-church-resolution-on-marriage.

---

[141] David Brooks, "The Next Culture War," New York Times, June 30, 2015. http://www.nytimes.com/2015/06/30/opinion/david-brooks-the-next-culture-war.html?rref=collection%2Fcolumn%2Fdavid-brooks

[142] Ibid.

[143] Ibid.

[144] Ibid.

[145] This study guide was prepared and written by The Rev. Andrew Parker, St. Timothy's Episcopal Church, Lake Jackson; The Rev. Mark Crawford, St. Luke's Episcopal Hospital, Houston; The Rev. Canon John Newton, Episcopal Diocese of Texas, Houston

[146] Sermon on Unity: http://www.sermoncentral.com/sermons/balanced-unity-charles-mallory-sermon-on-church-body-of-christ-147119.asp

[147] The conclusion was drafted by our Unity and Mission Task Force as support of the paper.

CPSIA information can be obtained
at www.ICGtesting.com
Printed in the USA
LVHW040020131118
596926LV00021B/1098